POOR BITOS

POOR BITOS

JEAN ANOUILH

Translated by LUCIENNE HILL

COWARD-McCANN, Inc. New York

CHARACTERS

BITOS, *who plays Robespierre*
MAXIME, *who plays Saint-Just*
PHILIPPE, *who plays the Jesuit Father*
JULIEN, *who plays Danton*
VULTURNE, *who plays Mirabeau*
BRASSAC, *who plays Tallien*
DESCHAMPS, *who plays Camille Desmoulins*
VICTOIRE, *who plays Lucile Desmoulins*
AMANDA, *who plays Madame Tallien*
LILA, *who plays Marie Antoinette*
CHARLES, *Maxime's butler*
JOSEPH, *Maxime's cook*
DELANOUE
CHILD ROBESPIERRE

ACT ONE

An immense room, vaulted and completely bare.
Stone steps upstage leading up and off to an un-
seen street door. Downstage a big trestle table
laid for several guests.

MAXIME, *dressed in a dinner jacket and carrying*
a lighted candelabrum, is showing PHILIPPE
around the room. He is wearing the wig and neck
linen of the French revolutionary period. PHI-
LIPPE *is in traveling clothes.*

MAXIME. This is the great hall. It's all that remains of the old
Carmelite Priory. The local Jacobins held their meetings
here in 1792. In '93 they set up the Revolutionary Tribunal
here.

PHILIPPE. What are you going to do with it?

MAXIME. (*Shortly*) Sell it. I'm signing next week with Shell.
Yes, my dear fellow, a garage. Ultra modern. Neon everywhere. With petrol pumps gleaming like graven images.
They'll pour cement into it all with whoops of glee. That
will teach my ancestors to let themselves be guillotined like
sheep. I loathe those tales of aristocrats who mounted the
scaffold smiling with contempt. Had they barricaded themselves in here and died fighting like men, I should have
preserved this edifice. But they listened nice and politely
to their death sentence, so—a garage!

PHILIPPE. Pity. It was lovely.

MAXIME. With neon lights it will be lovelier still. However,
as occasions for enjoying oneself are rare in the provinces, I
decided to have a housewarming before I sold the place.

7

PHILIPPE. (*Grunting*) A wig party! Nobody gives those any more. It's going to be lugubrious.

MAXIME. (*With a smile*) I fondly hope so.

> PHILIPPE *eyes him, surprised.*

PHILIPPE. How very cheering.

MAXIME. (*Taking his arm*) I'd better let you into the secret. I'm hatching a vast scheme for the ruination of an upstart who annoys me. That's the real reason for tonight's festivities. You remember Bitos at school?

PHILIPPE. Bitos?

MAXIME. That boring little scholarship boy who always came top. (*Reciting*) Latin prose—first prize, Bitos. Greek prose—first prize, Bitos. Mathematics—first prize, Bitos. It was our great end-of-term joke. We all howled the predictable results in chorus, to the despair of the reverend fathers, who were always threatening to expel us. They took good care not to, of course. With nothing but their one little scholarship boy, those saintly men could never have covered their costs.

PHILIPPE. Oh yes, I'm with you now. The one we called "Beastly Bitos." What became of him?

MAXIME. Deputy public prosecutor, my dear. One fine day, after the Liberation, when we'd all forgotten him, up he jumps as deputy public prosecutor. It was revenge, you see. He'd suffered so much from our lurid practical jokes. We'd taunted him often enough with being a washerwoman's son. Now let us so much as dabble in some unsavory affair —decadent lot that we are—and he could crush us in his iron glove. Vengeance arriving by the local bus, and on market day too, along with the pigs and chickens, with his gray knitted gloves and his little attaché case crammed full of principles.

PHILIPPE. A zealot, is he?

MAXIME. That's putting it mildly. He thinks he's Robespierre. Ever-present Justice is on the march and he is it, with that mock-leather briefcase he totes about everywhere. Our corrupt little city will have to behave itself or else. You've noticed my wig and ruffles? Do I look deadly enough? I'm supposed to be Saint-Just. The joke is, I'm told it's very like. This evening, we're back in 1793. The guests are all coming as figures of the period and they've made a thorough study of their roles. And mind, there's to be no discussing anything else all evening, that's an order. We must have our facts at our fingertips. That nitwit Julien has been boning up his revolutionary history for a fortnight.

PHILIPPE. But my dear boy, we're going to be bored to tears at your little historical evening.

MAXIME. (*With a wicked smile*) No, you won't. The bill of fare includes a sentence of death and that's always fun. I've persuaded Bitos to come as Robespierre. Philippe, my boy, you won't regret your evening.

PHILIPPE. You know I've always been hopeless at history. I don't know that I'm too well qualified at this short notice.

MAXIME. My dear, I've reserved you Louis XVI. You've the profile for it and it's a virtually non-speaking role. As a matter of fact, you've only one line to say. "Is this a revolt?" "No, Sire, it's a revolution." Can you remember that? Come along. We're going to paint and powder you.

PHILIPPE. And you think Bitos dressed up as Robespierre and holding forth will be enough to liven up your little surprise party, do you?

MAXIME. The fellow can't hold his liquor. And—it's a big word and I loathe big words—but the fact is I hate him. He won't leave my little surprise party, as you call it, alive.
    He repeats, lifting a finger with a smile, suddenly strange:
Not alive.
    Enter CHARLES, *the manservant, white-coated, with a period wig.*

9

This is Charles, whom you know but possibly don't recognize.

CHARLES. Sir.

MAXIME. Our friends will be arriving any minute, I asked them all to get here before the guinea pig.

PHILIPPE. But suppose the guinea pig suspects something and doesn't come at all?

MAXIME. (*Leading him off*) That breed are much too sure of themselves ever to suspect a thing. I asked him for nine o'clock. At one minute to nine—the breed is always early—he'll be here.

> *They go out.* CHARLES *starts to light the candles on the table. A knock. He goes up the steps to answer the door. Two young women and a young man, all in period wigs, appear at the top of the steps.*

LILA. Good evening, Charles. How do we look?

CHARLES. Marvelous, ladies. M. Maxime will be delighted.

LILA. (*Who is made up as Marie Antoinette*) I've gone to no end of trouble. My little edifice is a work of art. But it won't stay perched on my head until the dessert, that's certain.

JULIEN. (*Who is made up as Danton*) A point of no importance, dear girl, your role is comparatively short. They cut your head off before then.

LILA. (*Looking around her*) Maxime has some impossible ideas! Fancy inviting people to dinner in a cellar!

JULIEN. I've seldom been bored at a party of Maxime's. He has an astonishing sense of theatre. (*He looks at* CHARLES) Why, look at Charles, he's in it too!

CHARLES. (*Smiling with faint embarrassment*) A little fancy of M. Maxime's. He said I might be useful when the time came.

AMANDA. I rather fear that what Maxime wants us to do won't be very charitable, or very pretty either.

JULIEN. My love, this evening we've come here to have fun. Charity is for tomorrow morning, after Mass. But for tonight, let Charity sleep.

VULTURNE *appears at the top of the stairs, made up as Mirabeau.*

VULTURNE. Excuse me, the door was open. Is this the right house for the conspiracy? Marie Antoinette, if memory serves?

LILA. The Count of Mirabeau?

VULTURNE. (*With a mock bow*) Thank you, your Majesty. I was afraid there might be some doubt. That's why I've been very lavish with the pockmarks. Do you like it? I've put them on every available inch. (*To* AMANDA) Good evening, Amanda. Dear God, aren't we pretty! Who are we exactly?

AMANDA. (*Reciting like a schoolgirl*) Theresa Cabarrus, known as Our Lady of Thermidor, who married Tallien, Member of the National Convention. It was because of her that Tallien brought matters to a head with Robespierre on the 8th Thermidor. It seems they cooked Robespierre's goose with a handbell.

VULTURNE. President of assassins! I demand to speak. Ting-a-ling! Ting-a-ling! I can't wait to hear our little Bitos shouting that.

JULIEN. Marvelous, that smallpox, Vulturne. I swear it's almost catching. Tell me honestly, do you think I look like Danton? Maxime picked the role out for me entirely because I spent my youth booting Bitos in the behind. He says the memory of it would help considerably to set the mood.

BRASSAC *appears. Tallien's head, feathered hat.*

BRASSAC. Good evening.

LILA. (*To* BRASSAC) Who are you supposed to be, Brassac?

One can tell that you're supposed to be something, but it isn't clear quite what.

BRASSAC. Tallien. An excellent role for a wig party. Nobody quite knows his true face. Yes, my dear, the turncoats, the putrefied of conscience, the traitors, they're me, rolled into one.

LILA. What an ugly role. Aren't you ashamed?

BRASSAC. No. You owe the turncoats of this world an almighty lot, let me tell you. They were the ones who decided at last to put a stop to the Terror and knock Robespierre off his perch. All they were concerned with was saving their skins and their fat purses. They were more surprised than anyone, on meeting the cheering mob outside the National Assembly, to learn that they had just saved France.

AMANDA. You mean they made fortunes during the Revolution? I thought everything had been given to the people.

> BRASSAC *puts his arm around her and kisses her familiarly on the neck.*

BRASSAC. Darling little Amanda. Why, my little dove, money was never made so fast as when they started bothering about the common people. It's become a veritable industry.

LILA. Bitos will be furious when he sees you here!

BRASSAC. I should hope so. What amazes me is that he should accept an invitation to dine with the forces of Capital. But he's the ambitious one, as it turns out. I was quite content to take over my papa's numerous factories. He didn't deign to carry on his mother's laundry business, not he. He got himself appointed deputy public prosecutor and began washing dirty linen on a grander scale.

JULIEN. Have you heard the latest Bitos story?

LILA. The one about the apartment he requisitioned for his sister on the same day he demanded the death penalty for the tenant on charges of collaboration? It was magnificent. You couldn't tell in the end what he was pleading for—the man's head or the apartment.

JULIEN. No, not that. The one about the boyhood friend he had sentenced to death in a fit of righteousness. Bitos had obtained the conviction of a young member of Laval's militia, arrested a good while after the Liberation. The boy had made his first communion with him and they'd been friendly, it seems, up until the war. All this was three years ago. Whether because of red tape, indecision, forgetfulness or I don't know what, the fact is that our humanitarian regime kept this boy in the condemned cell, in leg irons, for three years, watching for the dawn. Last week, they suddenly remember him and decide to execute him after all. Visit from the wretched fellow's wife, in tears, accompanied by their little girl. Bitos, more and more the noble Roman, weeps with her—and sincerely, too, I think—but doesn't yield an inch. Anyway, the matter was out of his hands. He's included, of course, in the little early morning expedition to see his fellow communicant peppered with bullets, wondering if he'll manage to keep his breakfast down. The other fellow, in a desperate bid to raise the tone of this final minute, asks to shake Bitos by the hand before walking to the execution post. Mutual forgiveness. He cries "Vive La France" very nicely and they allow him to shout "Fire" himself; so they duly shoot holes in his belly and lungs, some ten years after the offense. The deathshot fired, Bitos takes out his watch and says simply, "On time to the minute." A stationmaster! That night, he forks out and sends the little girl a doll—as a replacement, no doubt. A very expensive doll. That's the beautiful part. Bitos is a poor man. It cost him more than half his month's salary. A doll that opens and shuts her eyes, says Mama and Papa and does weewee. It was, in fact, a German doll; we're still executing people, but trade, of course, is well on its feet again.

LILA. You're determined to spoil our appetite, Julien my pet, that's perfectly obvious. How can you expect us to dine with Bitos after what you've told us?

JULIEN. (*Negligently*) My dear girl, if we had to respect all the people we dine with, there'd be no possibility of social life at all. Besides, Bitos isn't a murderer, he's a prosecuting counsel. In principle, he was only doing his duty.

> *A young man appears at the top of the steps; dark suit, bewigged and made up, looking rather ill at ease.*

YOUNG MAN. Excuse me. The door was open.

LILA. (*In a murmur*) This dinner party is certainly producing some surprising guests. Who's he?

JULIEN. (*Under his breath*) No idea.

YOUNG MAN. May I introduce myself? I'm Marcel Deschamps. M. Maxime de Jaucourt invited me here tonight. . . .

BRASSAC. (*Going to him*) I apologize for Maxime. The preparations for this little party are keeping him backstage. We haven't seen him ourselves yet. (*Introducing himself*) My name is Brassac. Let me introduce you. Monsieur Deschamps: the comtesse de Preuil, Mlle. Amanda Forrest, Julien du Bief.

VULTURNE. (*Introducing himself*) Verdreuil.

DESCHAMPS. (*Surprised*) Are you M. le comte de Verdreuil?

VULTURNE. Yes.

DESCHAMPS. We're not strangers then. I'm headmaster of the village school at Bréville.

VULTURNE. Really? I'm delighted to meet you; my game-keeper's two boys are with you. Their father tells me that since you've been in charge he hardly recognizes them. No doubt that's why he's stopped thrashing them every night.

DESCHAMPS. (*Smiling*). They're good boys and they've really got down to work now. They needed the right handling, that's all.

VULTURNE. (*With a charming bow*) And I see you know how to do that. Are you a friend of Maxime's?

DESCHAMPS. (*A little embarrassed*) I hadn't the honor of M.

Jaucourt's acquaintance until recently. He came to see me a fortnight ago and invited me to this little party. Perhaps because he assumed I knew a little history. He asked me to come as Camille Desmoulins. I've done my best.

LILA. (*Aside to* JULIEN) This party is getting more and more mysterious.

JULIEN. Maxime is a man of dark designs.

MAXIME *walks in quickly.*

MAXIME. Are you all here? I can't apologize enough, but I was making up our dear old friend Philippe as Louis XVI. M. Deschamps, have you been introduced?

DESCHAMPS. I introduced myself.

MAXIME. You know he's our schoolmaster at Bréville, Verdreuil?

VULTURNE. So he said.

MAXIME. M. Deschamps, you and André Bitos have known each other for years, I believe?

DESCHAMPS. (*Surprised and on his guard*) Yes. Very well. Especially as children.

MAXIME. He's coming here this evening. He picked the role of Robespierre and I asked you to come as Camille Desmoulins. In view of what happened between you—it remains your secret, don't worry—can you see any objection to your meeting?

DESCHAMPS. On the contrary, I'm delighted to be given the chance of telling André Bitos just what I think of him— under the mask of Camille Desmoulins . . .

MAXIME. (*Smiling*) Under the mask of Camille Desmoulins . . . I see we understand each other.

      He begins to pour drinks, speaking as he does so.
I want you to take your roles seriously, all of you, and not attack Bitos with anything but historical arguments, will you do that? No personal references, whatever you do. That would spoil everything.

JULIEN. (*Nervous, consulting his little book*) Will our history be up to it, though, that's the thing.

MAXIME. Don't worry, those fellows were great talkers. The problem was holding the floor for as long as you could. The least interruption was fatal. When they cut into your speeches they cut off your head as well. That was made very clear on the 9th Thermidor. How do you suppose they got Robespierre? By making enough noise to drown his voice. The second he couldn't talk any more, he was dead. Long live democracy, which gives us the spoken word.

JULIEN. Talking of that, have you got a handbell?

MAXIME. The murder weapon? I should think so!
He rings the bell. CHARLES *appears.*
All right, Charles, just testing. But I've something even better than that. The high spot of the evening, the deus ex machina who brings the play to a successful end. Merda, the gendarme. Angelic little Merda, who walked straight into the City Hall, asked which of them was Robespierre and then just drew his gun and shot him. So simple it was silly, but someone had to think of it.

AMANDA. (*Clapping her hands, delighted with her knowledge*) Why yes, that's another thing I learned last night. It's as exciting as a thriller. Who's to play Merda?

MAXIME. A very handsome young man, my angel, who won't arrive until the dessert.

LILA. Who is he? Do we know him?

MAXIME. I don't think so.

AMANDA. But why isn't he coming earlier? Did he have a previous engagement?

MAXIME. No, poor fellow. He has very few invitations these days. But I thought that his presence at the beginning of dinner might sour the proceedings somewhat prematurely.

VULTURNE. Ah, so you do mean to sour the proceedings, do you?

16

MAXIME. (*With a wicked smile*) Toward the end, yes. (*Suddenly cold*) Vulturne, you can always withdraw from this dinner party if you're afraid you'll weep over Bitos.

VULTURNE. (*Shrugging*) No. After all, it's only a romp and Bitos is a second-rate man. And I think God will forgive everybody except the second-rate.

MAXIME. Let's not be more forgiving than God, then, my dear Vulturne.

A knock.

Charles! The door! I hope to heaven it's Victoire. She absolutely must be here before he is. We can't do anything without a Lucile Desmoulins. Saved! She's here!

VICTOIRE *appears, and smiles and nods to everybody from the top of the stairs. She is wearing a period bonnet.*

VICTOIRE. Good evening. I'm the last, I'm sorry. Will you excuse me, there's something I must say to Maxime.
She draws him aside.

MAXIME. What's the matter?

VICTOIRE. Maxime, I can't stay this evening.

MAXIME. My darling Victoire, you can't ruin my party! I simply cannot do without you.

VICTOIRE. You'll see why when I tell you. Something quite unbelievable has happened. My father only told me about it just as I was leaving. Bitos came to see him this afternoon and he asked him for my hand.

MAXIME. That's splendid! Splendid! I did suspect that the fellow was vaguely paying court to you, that's why I asked you to come as Lucile Desmoulins. But I never dreamed I'd hit the target! (*He cries comically to the others*) I'm a clairvoyant!

VICTOIRE. I don't know what he can have imagined. I've seen him four times at home, on the four occasions when my father had to receive the prosecution members in his capacity as President of the Court. He was our guest and I was pleasant to him—as I was to everyone else. But for him to think for one instant that I'd even noticed him!

MAXIME. (*Bursting with delight*) It's too perfect! It's too, too perfect!

VICTOIRE. You know my father. He went for him, all beard and eyebrows—it must have been sheer carnage—and told him very brutally that the answer was no. He flatly refused even to mention it to me.
   MAXIME *dances her around gleefully.*
(*Freeing herself*) Maxime, stop pretending. You must see that I can't possibly join in this evening's game, it would be too cruel.

MAXIME. In the first place, my dear child, one can't be too cruel to fools. Besides, I need a Lucile Desmoulins or everything will be ruined. And that is that.

VICTOIRE. If at least I'd refused him myself! But my father was very harsh. Bitos will think he's committed some dreadful social blunder. He must be dying of shame and mortification.

MAXIME. Let him die of whatever he likes, so long as I can give my party. My darling Victoire! Must I go down on my knees to you? (*He does so*) You who are kindness itself!

VICTOIRE. That's just why. I can't do it.

MAXIME. (*Pettishly*) Be kindness itself to me then, and not to him.
   A knock.
Anyway, it's too late. He's here now. Charles, answer the door. Straighten your little bonnet, Lucile Desmoulins, and have no remorse. Children, onstage for Act One.
   He gets to his feet, turns his back to her and goes to the others.

MAXIME. Julien, do you know your part? The Prairial Laws?

JULIEN. 22 Prairial '94. Intensification of the powers of the Revolutionary Tribunal.

MAXIME. Well done. Nine out of ten.

LILA. (*Aside to him*) What's the matter with Victoire?

MAXIME. Nothing. A slight hitch, which is a real godsend, as it turns out. (*To the others*) Don't force the pace at first, just let it come. Then, as soon as he's had a drink or two, launch into the argument. He'll tighten his own noose. Pick up your glasses, let's not look as though we're waiting.

> BITOS *appears at the top of the stairs. He is dressed as Robespierre from head to foot, under his skimpy topcoat and bowler hat. When* CHARLES *takes his coat, he stands revealed in sky blue.*

BITOS. Excuse me, ladies and—

MAXIME. My dear Bitos, you're the last! Why, what on earth have you got on?

BITOS. (*Already on the defensive*) What do you mean? What is this, a practical joke? You're all in dinner jackets! You told me it was fancy dress!

MAXIME. (*Roaring with laughter*) A wig party! You misunderstood me, Bitos, or perhaps you weren't familiar with the custom. A wig party has nothing to do with a costume ball! My dear man, you only dress up your head!

> *Everyone laughs at* BITOS' *bewilderment.*

BITOS. (*Crushed*) I apologize. I must look ridiculous. I'll go home and change.

MAXIME. No, no, don't bother. You'd make us dine at an impossible hour. Anyway, sky blue suits you wonderfully. I'm sure the ladies will be enchanted to have you in blue. Now then, everybody. The game has begun. Don't forget, we aren't ourselves any more. You know nearly everyone, I think? Her Majesty, our Queen. The beautiful Madame Tallien. A gentle, virtuous young woman whom you loved very much, I believe—Lucile Desmoulins. The comte de Mirabeau. Your good friends Danton and Camille Desmoulins. Tallien, whom I understand you didn't care for. I got Brassac to play him, we needed someone really rich, didn't we? Have I forgotten anyone? Oh yes, of course! One always forgets him, poor thing, and nobody ever lets him speak. Gentlemen, the King!

> PHILIPPE *has come in. He is greeted with exclamations; the women sink playfully into deep curtsies as he passes.*

PHILIPPE. I'm not sure that it's a very good likeness. Anyway, I put as much powder on my head as it will hold.

MAXIME. You'll get it cut off so soon, why worry? Make your bow, Bitos! And politely, too. Whatever your present feelings, in '92 you were still a monarchist, remember.

BITOS. (*Banteringly*) A monarchist? Even after the King's death? He voted for it, didn't he? Correct me if I'm wrong.

MAXIME. Not for the Bourbons by then, no, of course not, but for himself. That, it seems, was why the Right Wing always kept a certain regard for Robespierre. They could feel the ruler in him. It's odd, isn't it, this French yearning for the iron fist? Basically, Robespierre for them was still law and order.

BITOS. This alleged collusion with the clergy and the Right, which certain historians have been pleased to insinuate— I can't think why—that's a point that needs to be discussed.

MAXIME. My dear fellow, that's what we're here for. Let's go in to dinner. You all have your little place cards.

> BITOS *bows to everyone, then strolls over to* DESCHAMPS, *very much at ease, while the company find their places at the table and* CHARLES *begins to serve.*

BITOS. Deschamps, it's good to see you after all this time. But I must say I'm surprised. I would never have guessed you were a friend of M. Jaucourt's.

MAXIME. Monsieur Deschamps is the schoolmaster at the village school at Bréville. M. de Verdreuil asked if he could bring him. I gather that you two were friends years ago.

BITOS. (*A trifle strained*) It's always nice to meet old friends. Are you still a schoolmaster? Why have you never shown signs of life since I've been appointed to the Courts here?

DESCHAMPS. (*Quietly*) You know why. Do you want to hear me say it again?

MAXIME. Do come and sit down, Bitos! Your soup will get cold. And don't forget, from this moment on you are Robespierre.

BITOS. (*Glancing along the table as he sits down*) There's an empty place.

MAXIME. Yes. Another friend of ours who's coming later. I have reconstructed a meal of the times for you. (*Turning to* BITOS) I mean before the austerity laws. . . . So I hope you'll enjoy your dinner. And eat a little too much as well.
A pause. They eat.

BITOS. (*Stiffly, as he takes the proffered dish*) I don't believe that the members of the Convention, the dedicated ones, were very interested in that kind of thing. Besides, times were terribly hard, don't forget that.

MAXIME. My dear man, in the midst of the worst catastrophes, the French have never once given up the thought of eating well. Those who could afford it, that is. I read somewhere that there was a very well organized black market at the time.

BITOS. (*Already a little tight-lipped*) I'm afraid it has always been virtually impossible, no matter how stringent the laws, to prevent the rich from polluting everything with their money. I don't say that some pleasure-seekers—the Dantons—the Talliens—

JULIEN. (*Ringing the bell, cries*) Easy now, Max my lad, you haven't guillotined me yet!

BRASSAC. (*Passing him the dish*) Help yourself while you can, then. When you're dead everything will be cold.

BITOS. (*With a pale smile at the interruption*) But Robespierre, I'm sure, never took part in those banquets. He lodged with a poor cabinetmaker and broke bread with him at the family table.

MAXIME. Oh yes, but that poor cabinetmaker had a cousin in the country who sent him the odd hunk of bacon; a crony employed in the countinghouses of the old West India Company who dipped into the stocks of coffee now and then. So take one of these plover's eggs, my dear fellow, and don't think badly of yourself.

BITOS. (*Helping himself primly*) Yes, on the occasion of a family celebration, I don't say that some didn't stretch a point and procure certain good things for themselves. After all, it's only human. But I am convinced that Robespierre, determined as he was to be incorruptible, did not share in their feasting.

AMANDA. "No thank you," he said, "I'm incorruptible. No roast lamb for me. Just beans."

BITOS. (*Trying to laugh*) Don't scoff, young lady! I meant that when those good folk indulged themselves, they probably took care he didn't know about it.

LILA. How horrid of them! Do you think they waited until he'd gone up to his room all by himself with his little bowl of broth?

BRASSAC. And they shouted at the children: "Don't crunch the bones, you little idiots! Robespierre will hear you!"

BITOS. (*With a jaundiced smile*) You have a very fanciful way of imagining history, my dear sir.

BRASSAC. To begin with, don't call me my dear sir. Call me citizen. And don't forget you used to address me by my Christian name. All those men, who handed one another over to the executioner, used to slap each other on the back and call each other by their first names. You called Danton Georges and Desmoulins Camille; both of whom dined with you the very evening before you clamored for their heads in the National Assembly. You called me Jean! The man you must have hated most.

BITOS. (*Pontificating*) A great band of friends they were, yes —but friends who didn't shrink from sacrificing one another on the way, so that the furrow plowed by their common love for the people should stay straight. I am amazed that you don't feel the grandeur of it, Brassac.

MAXIME. (*Pretending to interview him*) Monsieur Robespierre, would you say that the populace valued the grandeur of these men's sacrifice?

BITOS. (*Bitterly*) The people don't always value those who lead them along the thorny road of happiness.

MAXIME. (*Continuing the game*) I seem to detect a hint of bitterness in your words. Did you feel that the people did not care for you?

BITOS. (*Smiling affably and joining for the first time in the game*) They feared me. That was enough. I lived amongst them. I shared their discomfort and their poverty. Apart from this blue suit, my one conceit—I loathed sloppiness; I loathed disorder and dirt, it's true—I lived as they did.

JULIEN. (*Shouting from the other end of the table*) Hypocrite! All the Duplay women where you lodged petted and pampered you!

BITOS. (*Bristling*) Who called me hypocrite?

JULIEN. (*Leaping to his feet, his mouth full*) Your friend Danton! Danton the Big Mouth! Wait till I swallow. I've got my mouth full of friend Tallien's plover's eggs. For *I* loved good food, I did! I loved women, I loved life. And that's why you had me killed, you hypocrite! You thought you hated sloppiness, and disorder and dirt; it was the people you hated! And do you know why? Because they frightened you! And so did women—whence your purity—

and so did life. You killed us all because you didn't know how to live. We paid dearly for those complexes of yours.

BITOS. (*With a shrug, trying to make the others laugh*) Complexes, I ask you, in 1793!

JULIEN. You were a priest, Robespierre, that's the truth of it, a dirty little priest from Arras, all prim and proper, a nasty little snotty-nosed runt.

> BITOS *has half risen, nettled. One feels that* JULIEN *bawling at him frightens him rather as it did long ago.*

BITOS. I rather think you've overstepped the mark now, my dear fellow.

MAXIME. My dear Bitos, the game may be a little bitter, but let's play it like sportsmen. I'm sure you yourself were hardly more indulgent toward Danton.

BITOS. (*Sitting down again, balefully*) Danton was a hog! Sprawled out all night long with whores, he'd arrive at meetings in the morning, half dressed, stinking of cheap scent and drink. And one had to discuss the Revolution with that trash!

JULIEN. *My* Revolution smelled strong! Too bad for your precious little nostrils. When it went to fetch the King in October, do you think the Revolution didn't stink of female sweat and wine on the road to Versailles?

BITOS. (*Shouting*) Danton loved rioting, he didn't love the Revolution!

JULIEN. (*Turning comically to the others*) Give me something to drink or I'll do a murder! A murder that wouldn't even be historical! And to think I have to let them guillotine me first!

BITOS. Your verve, your audacity, your enthusiasm—they were all useful in their time. But there came a day when the Revolution had to rise above the sentimentality and the mob riots. That day, Danton became expendable. You should have realized that and kept quiet.

JULIEN. (*Rising and shouting as at a trial*) Jury of murderers, you shall listen to me! You'll not stop my mouth, any of you! The Revolution is my sister and my sweetheart. I know her, none better! I've lain with her.

BITOS. (*With a contemptuous shrug*) Phrases!

JULIEN. No! Cries! Real cries of men bursting from our guts, Camille's and mine. Cries of innocence which will haunt men's memories forever.

BITOS. (*Stiffly*) I heard nothing.

    JULIEN *eyes him steadily and says suddenly:*

JULIEN. Deaf too. It wasn't enough being shortsighted. You were deaf. Stiff and clumsy. With your fingers bunched at the ends of your stiff arms, you bumped into doors, knocking over chairs as you went, stepping on people's feet and too ill at ease to apologize. A dry little bit of clockwork without grace. A tightly wound automaton. Thin lips that never smiled, never kissed anyone, hands with bitten nails that had touched nothing ever—big staring eyes that never saw a thing. Without the Revolution, I could have been a wheelwright or a shoesmith; Camille could have played the harpsichord, or painted; Saint-Just could at least master a difficult horse. Even that poor fish Louis XVI wasn't a bad locksmith. If they'd sent him off to America as they talked of doing, he could probably have earned a living for himself and his family as well as most. But you, you couldn't do a thing with your hands. All you could do was talk. A nasty little lawyer. Do you remember what I said about you at the trial? The fool can't even boil himself an egg!

BITOS. (*With a hollow laugh*) Phrases! You died spouting words like a ham actor. I did at least die in silence.

JULIEN. (*Starting to eat again*) Because they'd broken your jaw. Otherwise you'd have talked like the rest of them. One always talks.

LILA. (*Suddenly, in the silence which has oddly fallen*) It must have been exciting, I should think, Danton's trial.

BITOS. (*Shrugging*) Good God, madam, what's a trial!

VULTURNE. (*Smiling*) Breathtaking, my dear. A big star beloved to the vast public and—a rare thrill lost to the theatre since Roman times—one they were actually going to kill. All the ladies wanted tickets. The house was nearly as glittering as at the trial of the King. Of course, it was less of a grand occasion than Louis XVI's trial with all the women of fashion fanning themselves and eating ices in the boxes. At Danton's trial it was less dressy. In the first place, it was no longer the done thing in '93. A lot of friends had lost their heads since then. The vogue was for simple little day dresses, a light half mourning. It had rather more the flavor of an avant garde piece for connoisseurs. The fascinating question was how Danton was to be stopped from speaking.

AMANDA. And how did they manage it?

VULTURNE. By passing a vote excluding all the accused from the proceedings on the grounds that they were insulting to the court. It was a masterstroke. This neat little vanishing trick permitted them to be condemned to death without a hearing. Every century or so French justice, rather backward in other respects, produces little inventions like this one, to help it out of difficult situations—deft little tricks of the trade which allow it to serve the regime, whatever it happens to be.

BITOS *has risen, ashen pale.*

BITOS. Maxime, this is going too far. I am a guest in your house and as a member of the judiciary I cannot allow—

VULTURNE. (*Very calmly*) Will you deny that this was the way poor old Danton was whisked off?

BITOS. (*Leaping up*) Whisked off! I realize that you are not a democrat, but there *was* a vote taken. A properly conducted vote. Danton's death was therefore a decision taken by France.

JULIEN. The things they manage to get France to say with a majority of twelve votes!

BITOS. (*Yelping*) A vote is a vote!

JULIEN. (*Ironically*) Alas.

BRASSAC. And that vote, my dear Robespierre, you could only get from us! It was by leaning over to the Right that you got Danton's head.

BITOS. (*Shouting*) I deny this slanderous allegation! Robespierre was never in collusion with the Right!

BRASSAC. How else could he have formed a majority? He knew his political onions, the sea green incorruptible! The 9th Thermidor, when he sensed he was doomed, he turned to us and cried: "You, the pure of conscience! It is to you I speak!" Pure of conscience—us! He *must* have felt queasy!

BITOS. That's a lie! Everything you've put forward is a lie! You're interpreting history—

BRASSAC. It's in the encyclopedia. I learned it all at school with you, when we were twelve.

JULIEN. (*Waving the book*) Pass him the little book and let him see for himself—it's all there.

> MAXIME *rings the handbell and makes them all sit down again.*

MAXIME. Gentlemen, gentlemen . . . We're going much too fast. If we move at this rate we'll get to Waterloo before the coffee and I haven't even thought of a Bonaparte! Besides, I feel we're boring the ladies. With all these high politics they haven't been able to say a word. The ladies played their part too, you know, and a very vital one it was.

> *He seizes a serving spoon from* CHARLES *as he passes and hands it to* LILA *like a microphone.*

Your Majesty, with the lapse of time, would you be gracious enough to tell our listeners your personal feelings on the sad incidents which marked your reign?

LILA. (*Into the microphone*) Well, we were most surprised, the King and I, at the turn events were taking. . . . We were a very united family. Louis was a good father, a good husband and—we were convinced of this—a good king. His concern for the well-being of his subjects was the most touching thing in the world. How many times, on coming home from a ball, did I find him, late at night, poring over his little red account book in his study, working out ways of economizing.

MAXIME. (*Still very much the radio interviewer*) There were some unfortunate rumors about you at the time, your Majesty. Could you tell the listeners whether there was any truth in them?

LILA. Yes and no. I was very young. I loved parties. I was very pretty. What young woman doesn't want to enjoy herself? Louis was very kind, very honest. He wasn't a very amusing man. I had friends.

MAXIME. And could one say, as was alleged, that those friends led you into doing one or two rather rash things?

LILA. What young woman isn't rash at some time in her life?

MAXIME. We won't mention the balls and parties particularly. . . . (*Into the microphone*) It is important to remember, ladies and gentlemen, that the pomp and splendor of the royal house was a real political necessity at the time. The people would have been the first to feel mortified if their King hadn't the finest diamonds, the finest palaces, the finest festivities—(*he bows gallantly to* LILA)—the loveliest Queen.

LILA. (*Simpering*) Thank you.

MAXIME. (*Still into the microphone*) This love, which they have since transferred to popular singers, footballers and film stars—this love they bestowed in those days on their King and Queen.

LILA. They're always talking about the money I spent, but I

set the simplest fashions. I used to wear muslins and cotton prints. The common people resented me for it, as a matter of fact. They detest simplicity. My extravagant follies? Combing my lambs on my little farm, milking my cow? I was the first Queen of France who took a delight in living like the humblest of her subjects. Well really, one can't say I was ruining France by milking Roussette! . . . that was my cow.

MAXIME. (*Banteringly into the microphone*) Her Majesty has just let us into an amusing little secret, her cow was called Roussette.

> BITOS *thrusts his face into hers. They are nose to nose, like two quarreling children.*

BITOS. The Trianon hamlet cost an outrageous fortune!

LILA. Everything cost us a fortune. You could hardly expect us to haggle with our tradesmen!

BITOS. What about your friends? What about the pensions?

LILA. I know. Everybody has always thrown Mme. de Polignac up at me. I loved her very dearly. I had every right to do it.

BITOS. You had no right to heap her and her family with riches! It was a downright scandal!

LILA. The Polignacs were very hard up. I had to help them, didn't I? Have you never helped a friend, sir?

BITOS. (*With a cry*) Never!
> *Everyone laughs.*

JULIEN. At last, a cry from the heart.

BITOS. (*Shouting, nettled*) Let me finish, will you? I really don't see what's so funny. Never, with the people's money—

LILA. (*Innocently*) Because you never had the spending of it.

BITOS. (*Bawling*) I did! And more freely than you did, possibly. I never lived in a palace. All I ever had were my attendance vouchers at the Committee and my salary from the Assembly. On the 9th Thermidor all they found in my house were fifty silver francs and I owed the Duplays four years' rent. Who else could boast a balance sheet like that? Danton, Mirabeau, Tallien even?

BRASSAC. (*Seriously*) My dear fellow, I was a financier. If I had had to produce accounts at any time, they would have been in order, you can be certain of that.

BITOS. (*Cackling*) I'm sure. And what about Mirabeau's pensions? He needed enormous sums of money. The inexhaustible needs of vice! We all know how much he got from the Court!

VULTURNE. (*Smiling*) I was a sincere royalist, my dear fellow. When convictions are genuine, it's somewhat specious to insist they shouldn't pay.

BITOS. (*Sneering*) Attractive principles.

VULTURNE. (*Smiling*) Pardon me. Lack of principles, which is quite a different thing.

BITOS. That's leaving the door wide open to grafters—to thieves!

VULTURNE. Possibly. But in politics France has often had occasion to note that they were less of a danger than the virtuous. It's a known fact, thieves do less killing. And if one has to choose—

BITOS. (*Outraged*) That's a vile thing to say, sir!

VULTURNE. (*Still smiling*) Yes, it's vile. Reality nearly always is. At least I can choose, if I have the choice, the form of vileness which costs me the least. Blood is the price one always pays for the haste of a few men like yourself who are impatient to play their little roles.

BITOS. Your cynicism is revolting.

VULTURNE. Possibly, but I'm gentle toward men, whose frailty I have accepted. And human tenderness, that lady whom you've never met, counts too.

BITOS. Human tenderness, as you call it, can consist of something other than indulgence and laxity! Remember what I shouted at the Convention when the fainthearted were talking about leniency. "Leniency for Royalists? Mercy for villains? No! Mercy for innocence! Mercy for the weak! Mercy for the unfortunate! Mercy for mankind!"

    Everyone applauds as in a public meeting, which disconcerts him a little.

VULTURNE. (*Retorts with a smile*) And very fine it sounded too. But I've observed that those who talk too often of mankind have a curious propensity for decimating men.

BITOS. Nature decimates, weeds out, and slaughters, too! Nature spawns and exterminates millions of creatures every day! A day in the life of the world is just one vast birth and one vast slaughter for the fulfillment of her plans.

VULTURNE. Possibly. But Nature's plan was not born in the brain of M. de Robespierre. Faced with an earthquake one can only bow the head, agreed. But when the earthquake has been conceived by a handful of petty intellectuals, one may be tempted to intervene—

BITOS. (*Shouting*) Are you preaching civil war?

VULTURNE. My dear man, I have a horror of bloodshed, but I do not, for all that, feel myself cut out to be a rabbit.

    BITOS *bangs on the table, forgetting himself.*

BITOS. (*Screeching*) Nothing will halt the march of progress! That's what enrages you. And when it comes to defending yourselves and your property, your side aren't so economical with blood then!

VULTURNE. Kings have massacred since the dawn of the world too. But they at least had the courage to say it was for the advancement of their affairs or for their own good pleasure. You and your like, while doing the same sort of work, lay your hands on your hearts. That's what I find repugnant in you.

BITOS. (*Has risen, very pale*) Monsieur, take that back.

VULTURNE. (*Filling his glass*) Too late. It's out. A little champagne?

> BITOS *has thrown down his napkin. He now affects a haughty calm and turns to* MAXIME.

BITOS. My dear Maxime, I knew if I came to your house that I should be alone in defending my opinions. I did think this exchange of ideas would be spirited but courteous. I see I was wrong. I must ask you to excuse me. Will you kindly send for my coat?

> MAXIME *has risen too.*

MAXIME. (*With a calm smile*). No.

BITOS. What do you mean, no?

MAXIME. My little party isn't over yet and you are indispensable. Charles will not give you your coat.

> BITOS *smiles a superior smile and takes a step toward the cloakroom.*

BITOS. Then I'll fetch it myself.

> MAXIME *and* JULIEN *bar his way.*

MAXIME. (*Still quietly*) You won't do that either. I assure you, Bitos, that we cannot do without you this evening.

BITOS. Is this a trap?

MAXIME. (*Laughing*) What a big word! It's a firm invitation.

BITOS. (*Looks at them and mutters*) What are you going to do to me?

MAXIME. (*Still calm*) Make you play your role to the end, that's all.

BITOS. (*Yelping*) You don't think I'm going to sit here and be your whipping boy with a good grace, do you?

MAXIME. It would be better, Bitos, if it were with a good grace.

> BITOS *goes to sit on a couch, pale but calm, and folds his arms.*

BITOS. Very well. Do what you like. This town is rotten with fascists and reactionaries, I knew that. I came with no illusions, but I did at least think I would be protected whilst under your roof by the laws of hopitality—if not honor. I know they talk a lot about honor in your world.

MAXIME. I promise you that honor, as far as I'm concerned, will be intact.

BITOS. (*With a mirthless laugh*) We know your methods. My compliments, ladies. I see the young women of your class have wholesome and innocent amusements. (*Suddenly glaring at* VICTOIRE) Mademoiselle de Brèmes, you are the only person whose presence here surprises and pains me. I suppose it was to punish me for daring to ask your father for your hand in marriage.

VICTOIRE. (*Murmurs, very pale*) I thought it would just be a harmless joke . . .

BITOS. (*Cackling*) And as you see, it is not a harmless joke.
He turns to the men, very dignified but slightly absurd.
Have you decided to eliminate me? I am a deputy to the Public Prosecutor and the Republic still exists. This may cause a stir in town tomorrow.

MAXIME. (*Bursting into laughter*) Don't be an ass, Bitos. Nobody's going to eliminate you. We need you too much to have fun with. Do you remember at school how we locked you in the dormitory and tossed you in a blanket? You came out of that with a few bruises and some skin off your nose. It didn't kill you.

BITOS. (*Bitterly*) And the reverend fathers finally conceded that you were only reviving a good old college custom— rather boisterous as amusements go—but in the great tradition, very Old World, very French. Don't imagine that the police and the law courts will be content to stop your chocolate money. This is an established criminal offense! (*He yelps absurdly*) Intent to inflict bodily harm! Article 132!

MAXIME. You see what comes of knowing too much law. You dramatize everything, Bitos. We haven't laid a finger on you yet. Don't tell me you're a coward?

BITOS. No.

MAXIME. No. One must be fair. I don't think you are. I'm sorry you aren't. (*He says heavily, between clenched teeth*) I loathe you, Bitos. I've loathed you ever since I was a small boy.

BITOS. (*Heavily too*) I know. I tried with all my might to be your friend. I made myself your slave. I carried your things, so that you could be free to run about. I never ran. All I ever got from you were snubs.

MAXIME. (*Softly*) I didn't like you.

BITOS. (*Murmurs, without looking at him*) Why didn't you?

MAXIME. You lacked grace.

BITOS. (*After a very slight pause*) You're the only one whose dislike ever hurt me. Everybody hated me at school because I always came first—and because I was a washerwoman's son! That's why they took me in for nothing. She washed your sheets, you little perverts—she washed your stained sheets for twenty years! It's those scrubbed-out stains that have made me what I am—Doctor at Law and Philosophy, Bachelor of Science, Mathematics, Letters, History, German —(*He yells, unaccountably*)—and Italian! Funny, isn't it? I passed every examination it was possible to pass. When the others went off for a beer after lectures I went back to my room and sat over my books. And when they came back late at night, after their evenings out with girls, I was still at it. Until the markets started and I went to help unload the lorries. After that I slept three hours—when I had three left. And at the first lecture, there I was again, the first in my seat, in the front row, with my silly great eyes open wide, to steal as much as I could of that precious bourgeois knowledge that my mother's soapy arms were paying for. (*He adds, calmer now, with a curious little gesture, venomous and yet prim*) If ever I'm entitled to a family crest like you, gentlemen, it will have my mother's two red arms upon it—crossed.

> A *silence follows this. Then* VULTURNE *says gently:*

VULTURNE. What became of your mother, Bitos?

BITOS. (*Stiffly*) She's dead. The sheets got her in the end.

VULTURNE. I'm sorry. I knew her. She was a brave woman.

> BITOS *bows ceremoniously, with a thin smile.*

BITOS. Thank you, your Grace, as they say in melodramas. Your mother was a fine woman too. I know that she helped mine, when my father died.

VULTURNE. (*After a pause*) I don't take back anything I said, Bitos, but I respect your courage and your integrity. I'm sorry if I hurt you. It only goes to prove that political discussion is always very difficult in France. In any event, MAXIME's game could lead to no good. I think they should let you have your coat.

MAXIME. I'm sorry, but there are a few of us here—aren't there, M. Deschamps?—for whom the memory of Bitos' mother, touching though it is, is not enough to wipe out certain things. Robespierre, the real one, had a mother, too, I imagine. Like all the men he sent to the guillotine, in fact.

> DESCHAMPS *steps forward.*

DESCHAMPS. (*Quietly*) While we're on the subject of your mother, I'm going to tell my story after all. When you demanded the death penalty for Lucien—who made his first communion with us, remember?—his mother came to see you the night before the trial, with yours. Those two old women knelt at your feet and clasped your knees and begged you to relent. And your mother wept as much as Lucien's did.

BITOS. (*Stonily*) He was a traitor.

DESCHAMPS. (*Quietly*) You and I were in the same Resistance group, Bitos, and every night we used to clench our fists, both of us, and say: "When it's all over, we'll get Lucien, we'll get him!"

BITOS. (*With a malicious smile*) So you admit it?

DESCHAMPS. Yes. But I should have settled it with fists, as we did years ago, in the schoolyard. Not with twelve rifles pumping lead into his guts at point-blank range, ten whole years later.

BITOS. Lucien fought against us. He'd killed men.

DESCHAMPS. (*In a murmur*) So had we.

BITOS. (*Screeching*) Are you comparing that little traitor's work with ours?

DESCHAMPS. No. We've had this argument before, the night our friendship died. All I wanted to say, since you brought up the memory of your mother, was that she pleaded with you, on her knees, for the best part of the night, and then at dawn, when she saw that her son was a true blue Roman, she got to her feet, did good old Mother Bitos, and with her big red washerwoman's hand she hit our hero twice across the face, hard.

BITOS, *very pale, half touches his cheek.*

BITOS. Very delicate of you, I must say, bringing up that grotesque incident.

DESCHAMPS. Not very delicate, no. Since the war, I've given up being delicate. But as you've chosen to hide behind your mother's skirts, I just wanted everyone to know what *she* thought of you, too.

BITOS. (*Looking round at them like a trapped animal*) Beatings, always beatings—everybody's always wanted to beat me. (*He cries out*) All right then, go on, beat me. There are six of you and I'm alone, what are you waiting for?

MAXIME. (*Coldly to the others—one must not know whether he means it or whether he is still only trying to frighten*

BITOS) I won't keep the women here, nor anyone else who no longer finds the game amusing. Charles, you may bring coats for anyone who asks for them. Except M. Bitos.

Everybody looks at one another anxiously. PHILIPPE *steps forward, trying to make a joke of it.*

PHILIPPE. Now, now, what's this—a revolt?

MAXIME. (*Smiling, says coldly*) No, Sire. It is a revolution.

PHILIPPE. (*More serious*) Maxime . . . I haven't said anything yet. You made me put a wig on the second I arrived, after an eight-hour drive. I haven't even had a chance to speak my one line, and I've hardly had any dinner. You've led me to expect more generous hospitality. I think you should let Bitos go if he wants to, and then you should serve us the rest of that fabulous meal of yours.

LILA. (*Stepping forward*) Maxime dear, we can't waste a whole evening like this. You surely aren't going to send us home at ten o'clock?

AMANDA. (*Taking his arm*) Maxime darling, now you're being ridiculous. You tried to make M. Bitos angry. You've succeeded. M. Bitos is angry. Now let him go home and let's finish our dinner.

MAXIME *grips her by the arm and shouts.*

MAXIME. Are you sorry for him?

AMANDA. Perhaps.

MAXIME. Women are always sorry for the wounds they haven't inflicted themselves. All right then, if you're sorry for him, kiss him.

He pushes them roughly toward each other.

AMANDA. Maxime! Are you mad?

MAXIME. Kiss him! Can't you see the way he's been looking at you? Kiss him, and I'll let him go.

He holds them forcibly together.

They smell good, rich women, eh, little priest? But when you ask for young girls' hands in marriage, you get thrown out of the house, and if you want to go to bed with the others, you'd better start making yourself attractive. So kiss her, you virgin! I must see you in a woman's arms before I die.

> *The others rush forward to free them from his grip.*

LILA. Maxime, you're abominable.

VULTURNE. (*Coldly, stepping forward*) I'm very fond of a joke, but I don't think this one is funny. We're all leaving. But we're not going without Bitos. I don't like him any more than you do, and I don't know what you were thinking of doing, but don't count on me to help you. There are some things that simply aren't done, that's all.

> *A pause.*

MAXIME. You may be sure he'll have far fewer scruples when he sends you to the firing squad. Bring the coats, Charles. M. Bitos' too.

> CHARLES *has hurried out to get the coats. He comes in a moment later, comically laden with garments. Everyone onstage has remained motionless and silent.*

CHARLES. Here we are . . . I hope you'll forgive me, ladies and gentlemen. I may get a little muddled up. . . . (*He says nervously to himself*) Ladies first. I think this one belongs to Mlle. de Brèmes. Excuse me, Mademoiselle. . . .

> *He hands her the coat, muttering.*

As a rule I have a system. I never allow it to form a bottleneck, but it's been so rushed with everybody leaving at once like this. This is M. le Comte's. . . .

> *He hands* VULTURNE *a coat clearly far too small for him.*

Oh no! Beg pardon, sir, my mistake. In thirty years I've never once done such a thing. This is yours. No, it's not! What a muddle! I'll never sort it all out on my own.

> *Nobody seems at all inclined to help him. He mutters. He goes out and calls:*

Joseph! Come and give me a hand! The ladies and gentlemen will excuse your attire, in view of the confusion.

> *The* KITCHEN BOY *appears, bewildered, in his blue-striped apron.*

Everybody's leaving at once. It's a stampede! Look for the ladies' cloaks.

> *The game goes on for a moment, a comic little piece of dumb show between the two servants, until the audience can stand it no longer, and at that instant the door into the kitchen opens and a* YOUNG MAN *comes bursting in. He is wearing a belted raincoat and an odd two-cornered gendarme's hat of the period. He halts in the doorway and says simply:*

YOUNG MAN. What about me, then?

> *They all turn in surprise. He goes on, a tense smile on his thin lips.*

What about Merda the policeman? Forgotten him in the kitchen, have we? Isn't he needed any more?

> *They all look at him blankly.* BITOS *instinctively steps back. He is deathly white.* MAXIME *stands frozen-faced. The* YOUNG MAN *looks at* BITOS *and says quietly:*

The 9th Thermidor—remember? Aren't we doing it now?

LILA. (*Crying out suddenly*) Maxime, who is this man?

YOUNG MAN. (*Stopping her with a gesture*) Introductions would take too long. And the only person concerned doesn't need one. Taller and a little thinner, aren't I?

BITOS. (*Getting the words out with difficulty*) You've escaped?

YOUNG MAN. (*Smiling*) It takes a magistrate to imagine you can escape from city jails. You asked for the maximum, remember, ten years. But even so, five seemed sufficient to the court. A year awaiting trial and the rest in the cells because, thanks to the length of the inquiry, I was just old enough to be considered a man. Sentence served, with a year off for good behavior, right? You can check up. I've done my time.

BITOS. (*Turning to* MAXIME) You brought this man here, didn't you?

MAXIME. (*Softly*) I needed a Merda. I couldn't think of anybody better for the part.

BITOS. (*Crying out nervously*) My conscience is clear! I only did my duty. He deserved no pity. A little postwar thug who hadn't even the excuse of poverty. You stole a car and you walked into a post office clutching a gun, like a gangster in a bad film.

YOUNG MAN. (*Quietly*) Exactly like a bad film, yes. But it's amazing how one's artistic sense develops in jail. These few years of solitude have given me a chance to realize the poor taste of what I did. So I have to thank you for playing an important part in the neglected education of a youngster who was—am I right?—utterly unknown to you.
He stresses these last words. A pause.

BITOS. (*Dully*) Yes, I knew your father. They say I owed my first promotion to him. I'm not denying it. I was his secretary at the County Court for a time. But that didn't affect the issue—just because you were the son of a former official in this town!
He shouts vengefully, his face twisted with hate.
Who is in jail himself as a collaborator! Is it my fault if your mother let you roam about the streets like a hooligan? I wasn't in charge of you! I only did my duty. I have nothing but loathing and contempt for little boys who hold up post offices after school, I'm sorry.

VULTURNE. (*Going to him*) Franz Delanoue. I remember you now. Yours is an appalling story, and they made you pay dearly for your childish prank, I know. But you're a man now. Come along, we're all leaving.

He takes his arm, but the YOUNG MAN *frees himself gently.*

YOUNG MAN. Just a moment. I was supposed to play Constable Merda. They arrested me once for playing at robbers. I want to play at cops now, to rehabilitate myself. (*He smiles*) That's all I know how to do—play. They never taught me anything else.

> *He starts to walk slowly over to* BITOS *through the crowd.* VULTURNE *makes a move but* MAXIME *holds him back, as he stands there, staring in fascination like the others, like* BITOS *too, while the* YOUNG MAN *comes slowly forward.*

. . . And Constable Merda walked through the crowd in the City Hall. He went straight up to Robespierre. "Are you Citizen Robespierre? I arrest you."

BITOS. (*Murmuring as if in a dream*) You're a traitor! I am going to arrest *you.*

YOUNG MAN. (*Finishing the sentence with a thin smile*) . . . Said Robespierre. But Constable Merda, who wasn't much of a talker, saw no point in saying anything else and he drew his pistol—

> *The* YOUNG MAN *has pulled a gun from his raincoat pocket, a silly little period pistol, and he suddenly aims it at* BITOS, *who has been staring at him as if mesmerized. A shot.* BITOS *clutches his jaw. A woman screams. They all rush forward. Too late. Sudden blackout. Voices in the darkness.* "Who was he? The little hoodlum! A doctor! Get a doctor quickly! Keep calm, all of you! The gun wasn't loaded! But he's bleeding! Lie him down on the table. . . ." *Over the hubbub,* MAXIME's *voice is heard shouting to the* YOUNG MAN.

MAXIME. You get out of here! Go on, get out, I tell you. I'll take over now.

When the lights go up again at the end of this speech, the room is the same, but a strange pale daylight falls from the high window onto the table, now cleared of cutlery, where ROBESPIERRE *is lying. In a corner, two men in red caps of liberty appear to be on guard. Later, but not yet, we will recognize* CHARLES *and the* KITCHEN BOY. *They are playing cards on a stool. Suddenly* JOSEPH *stops playing and goes to the table where* ROBESPIERRE *is lying motionless, automatically staunching blood from his jaw from time to time.*

CHARLES. Is he dead?

JOSEPH. (*Coming back*) No. He's still moving. He's just wiped the blood off his mouth.

CHARLES. Are we going to have to stand guard over him all night?

JOSEPH. Yes, use your head, man! Four o'clock in the morning is no time to start guillotining people. This is the Age of Equality. They'll guillotine him at noon. Like everybody else.

He stuffs a wad of tobacco in his mouth. The other lights his pipe and they go on with their game, laying down their winning cards as

THE CURTAIN FALLS

ACT TWO

Same set. The two men are still playing cards. The light has changed. One of them takes a gulp of wine from a bottle, goes to take a look at ROBESPIERRE *and comes back again.*

CHARLES. (*Shuffling the cards*) Is he dead?

JOSEPH. No. He's still breathing.

CHARLES. If they wait till noon, they won't even be able to show him to the people.

JOSEPH. You can't be sure. Look at Osman, in that batch from Bicêtre. Stabbed himself with a nail, the old devil—bad business that, for the warder. They revived him a bit and they still managed to guillotine him alive—by rushing things a bit.

CHARLES. I tell you they'll have to get a move on with this one. I know a dying man when I see one.

JOSEPH. They have a tougher hide than you'd think, some of them. I was turnkey over at the "Force" in September '92 when they liquidated the prisoners. Rough day of it we had. Oh, did we sweat! A whole day, killing in the blazing sun. I must say the ladies in the neighborhood took pity on us though. They brought us pitchers of cider—you could still get it in those days.

CHARLES. (*Sighing*) We didn't know our luck.

JOSEPH. (*Bitterly*) Yes. Anyhow, as I was saying, about some having a tough hide. . . . Well, there was one I saw. He was a nonjuring priest. I lift my hatchet and I bash him one full in the face. He turns around, grabs me by the throat, and he starts to throttle me—with his skull split wide open, the bastard! (*He adds indignantly*) A priest, man! Spurting all over the place, it was. I was covered in it.

CHARLES. Your wife must have said a thing or two when you got home!

JOSEPH. She knew you couldn't keep clean killing all day. She dressed me according. But it was our little Louison, my youngest. She'd just come back from the country from my brother's farm. When she sees me coming in like that, guess what she says? A real gem it was. "Dada," she says, "you've killed the pig! Shall we have sausage for supper?" *They both laugh. He wipes away a little tear.* Parson sausage! The things they think of, the little innocents. (*Carrying straight on*) I must say, for meat I'd say '92 was probably the worst year of the lot.

CHARLES. Do you reckon it's better now, then?

JOSEPH. For those that haven't got relations in the country . . . it's tough. And to think that's what we stormed the Bastille for.

CHARLES. You were there, were you, at the Bastille?

JOSEPH. (*After a slight pause*) N-no. Were you?

CHARLES. (*Equally cautious*) No. Mind you, everybody couldn't be there. I mean, you couldn't have moved! But I know some that got themselves fake certificates to say they were there, like. And they've done all right for themselves! At one time there were no jobs going except for Bastille men.

JOSEPH. I don't mind telling you, I used to say I'd been there myself.

CHARLES. Me too.

JOSEPH. (*In a confessing mood*) And as for fake certificates, I'll not tell a lie, I'd got one.

CHARLES. (*Winking*) Me too. (*Suddenly man-of-the-world as he picks up the cards*) And when they transferred you to the Committee, it was a step up for you, was it—after being a turnkey?

JOSEPH. In a way, yes. It was better thought of. But over at the "Force," if you know when to look the other way, the night before executions, say, with people wanting to say good-bye to their friends, you could make yourself some good tips. And if it's true what they say, that there's to be no more executions now old Robespierre's dead, I know some who'll feel the pinch, in the prison service.

CHARLES. I don't care what they say, those folk had the tipping habit. So now the aristocrats are finished, who's left for your prisons? The Girondins? That was a flash in the pan. They expected a decent yield out of it, but it fizzled out. Danton and his friends, same thing. . . . It made a stir because Danton was a great chinwagger and he'd been talked about a lot, but it wasn't any too productive, that. And anyway, the whole movement of the thing came from Robespierre. Now he's dead. Next thing you know they'll be emptying the jails.

JOSEPH. (*Worriedly*) You may be right. . . .

CHARLES. To begin with, the people have had enough of the guillotine!

> He darts an anxious look at the prone figure of
> ROBESPIERRE *and goes on darkly.*

There's been protests. It began with the Rue St.-Honoré. What with the tumbrils going past the whole time—well, I mean! It was upsetting trade! Now it's the districts where the cemeteries are that won't stand for it. People are thinking it isn't healthy, with all those corpses. They're afraid of epidemics. Well, you can't blame them. They've got kids, too. The pits were brimming over.

JOSEPH. They put lime in, I heard.

CHARLES. Lime doesn't do anything, it still stinks. So then, starting with Danton, they took the bodies over to Monceaux. But they didn't plan big enough—it's always the same in France, no vision, they think small, it's full already. And they've started making a fuss in that quarter, too. I mean to say, executions are one thing, but you can't go thumbing your nose at the public.

JOSEPH. (*Looking at* ROBESPIERRE) Hello, your customer just moved.

CHARLES. With a bit of luck, they'll kill him alive. Are you going along?

JOSEPH. (*Shrugging*) Puh, executions . . . There's not the same excitement you got at the beginning. My wife, in the early days, she was crazy for it. First thing in the morning, off she went with her knitting to get herself a good seat. The housework used to suffer. She grew bored with it, like everybody else.

> ROBESPIERRE *has suddenly sat up and gone to throw himself into a nearby armchair. The two men jump up.*

CHARLES. Hey, citizen! Where do you think you're going?

ROBESPIERRE. I don't want to lie down any more.

CHARLES. (*To* JOSEPH) Shall we let him?

JOSEPH. Poh, they didn't tell us to stop him sitting down. But you try escaping, citizen, and we'll stick to our orders.

ROBESPIERRE. (*Says quietly with a faint smile*) Where do you suppose I could run to?

JOSEPH. True. It's guarded here. Not like last night's mess up at the City Hall.

ROBESPIERRE. (*Looking around him*) How did they get me here?

JOSEPH. On a plank.

ROBESPIERRE. (*Unexpectedly*) What have I done to you?

CHARLES. To us? Nothing.

ROBESPIERRE. (*With a vague gesture*) To them?

CHARLES. (*With a like gesture*) That's politics. Danton hadn't done anything to us either. We do what we're told. Seems it's Citizen Tallien who's in command now. What do you expect us to do about it?

ROBESPIERRE. I should like some water to stop the bleeding. *The two men look at each other.*

CHARLES. I'll see if I can find a basin. Keep an eye on him.

ROBESPIERRE *remains alone with* JOSEPH, *who paces about a bit, then settles himself astride a chair and goes off to sleep.*

ROBESPIERRE. (*Softly*) I shan't speak. They'll never hear my voice again. Danton shouted right until the last. Right until the last he mouthed theatrical phrases so that men would repeat them afterwards. Play actor! Not me. They'll never know what I was thinking, from the moment that young ruffian fired his gun full in my face. I looked at him as he pulled the trigger. It's odd, I had plenty of time to look at him. He wasn't yet twenty. He was as handsome as a god. I almost took him for Saint-Just. I didn't move. I let the pain open in me, suddenly like a great red flower. It was acute but it didn't last long and very soon I was at peace on that table where they'd laid me down. At peace for the first time.

> A *pause.* JOSEPH *is snoring now, on his chair.*
> ROBESPIERRE *goes on softly.*

All the noise, the fury and the agitation, the hatred and the hurts—gone with a pistol shot, and here was everything setting itself to rights. As my blood ebbed away through the hole in my jaw, I felt, one by one, all my other wounds close up inside me. Just a little more blood, a little more life still left, and then I would be cured, at last.

> A *pause. He adds mysteriously:*

It all falls into place. But it took a long time to learn.

> The CLASS MASTER *of the college—a Jesuit priest who has the same features as the King—and the*

child ROBESPIERRE *enter upstage. It is the grown-up* ROBESPIERRE *who speaks the little boy's lines, without appearing to notice the Jesuit Father.*

MASTER. (*Holding the canes in his hand*) Robespierre, you are an excellent pupil, but you are not respectful enough.

ROBESPIERRE. I obey in everything, Father.

MASTER. Your mind is not respectful enough. There is something rigid in your mind which disquiets me. We will teach you pliability.

ROBESPIERRE. Yes, Father.

MASTER. You say yes and something in your mind is saying no. We will not rest content with your apparent submission, Robespierre. We will chastise you until your mind says yes.

A *pause.*

ROBESPIERRE. How will you know, Father?

MASTER. (*Softly*) For that question, Robespierre, you will have ten extra strokes of the birch. Now, I shall answer it. We shall know when we no longer feel uncomfortable with you. You are a little scribbler, Robespierre. You are here out of charity, because your poor father served us loyally during his lifetime as judge of the Ecclesiastical Court. You are by far our best pupil, and yet we are obliged to punish you. You know why Father de Breteuil prescribed those ten strokes of the birch, plus ten from me for your insolent question just now? Undo your clothes, if you please.

ROBESPIERRE. (*Beginning to undress*) Yes, Father, I know why.

MASTER. The very tone of your reply shows that you do not know. Or rather that you do not want to know. You are going to be whipped, Robespierre, because you are poor and are making it a cause for pride.

ROBESPIERRE. Yes, Father.

MASTER. Turn around. Settle comfortably under my arm. You are going to be whipped for your obstinate insistence in always coming first. Because we know very well that every first prize you wrench from us is an act of revenge on the part of your pride, to make us pay for our charity.

ROBESPIERRE. Yes, Father.

MASTER. Turn around. Settle comfortably under my arm. We will either break our canes, Robespierre, or your spirit.

> *He whips him vigorously.* CHILD ROBESPIERRE's *face remains impassive.* ROBESPIERRE *himself has slowly risen from his chair, his face deathly pale.*

The other boys beg for mercy, the proudest of them lets out a cry. We will break your silence, too.

> CHILD ROBESPIERRE *begins to do his clothes up in silence. The* MASTER *studies him for a moment or so. A bell rings in the distance.*

It is nearly time for the visit from our Lord Bishop, who will certainly congratulate you on your remarkable composition in Latin verse. After your little triumph you will come back to my study, bare that ludicrous part of your anatomy where we have placed shame, and receive the ten strokes which I still owe you.

ROBESPIERRE. Yes, Father. Have I leave to go now?

MASTER. (*Gazing at him*) I should like to make a human being of you, Robespierre. I should like to prise some little failing out of you. You have my permission to beg for forgiveness and the remission of your punishment. I am quite prepared to examine your request favorably in view of that Latin verse composition which is going to bring honor to our college.

> *A short pause.*

I am not asking you for a painful demonstration. A word would do.

> *Another pause.*

After all, you are very young. . . . You have perhaps not

quite understood why I have seen fit to inflict this additional punishment on you?

ROBESPIERRE. (*Quietly*) Yes, I have, Father.

MASTER. Very well. You may go back to your class. I shall expect you in my study after his Lordship's visit.

He throws down the cane with a hint of pique.

This cane is wearing out. I must put in for a new one.

CHILD ROBESPIERRE *goes off toward his classroom. The* MASTER *watches him go and calls after him gently.*

Robespierre! If you forget to come, I have a great deal to do now with term ending, I might very well forget too. . . .

CHILD ROBESPIERRE *turns at the door.*

ROBESPIERRE. (*Simply*) I shall come, Father.

He goes out. The MASTER *suddenly clasps his hands and says:*

MASTER. O Almighty God, lighten this child's burden of pride.

He crosses himself and goes out on the opposite side.

Left alone, ROBESPIERRE *walks over to the birch, looks at it, touches it with his foot, then picks it up gingerly with a sort of frightened curiosity and sets it down again. He goes to pick up* BITOS' *bowler hat and little black overcoat which are lying in a corner. He puts them on and goes to sit timidly on the edge of a chair. He seems to be waiting apprehensively for someone. He gets up and says in a drained voice, like someone reciting a speech:*

ROBESPIERRE. I am a young deputy from . . .

His voice dies away with shyness. He sits himself down on the edge of his chair again, and settles down to wait. Suddenly MIRABEAU *walks in swiftly, in a dressing gown, elegant and spry for all his weight. He is utterly at ease, which makes an even greater contrast with* ROBESPIERRE.

MIRABEAU. (*Holding out his hand*) Have I kept you waiting, young man? I was receiving a charming and rather soporific delegation. The ladies of the Paris markets came to bring me fruit and fish to congratulate me on my speech. (*He smiles*) As you see, the job of a public man carries some small advantages: one gets fed.

> *He graciously waves him to a seat.* ROBESPIERRE *sits down stiffly.*

You wanted to see me?

ROBESPIERRE. (*Beginning his prepared speech*) Sir, I am a young deputy from the Constituent Assembly where I represent the Arras division—

MIRABEAU. Oh yes! You wrote to me. Maximilien de Robetierre.

ROBESPIERRE. (*Correcting him*) Robespierre.

MIRABEAU. (*With a smile and a gracious wave of the hand*) Robespierre, yes, of course. Forgive me. I have a poor memory for names, but I never forget a face. Have you made a speech yet?

ROBESPIERRE. I had the honor of intervening in the debate of the 30th May.

MIRABEAU. (*Kindly*) So you did. They didn't pay much attention to you. Voice a little weak, diction rather shaky still . . . I must give you a few tips. We must resign ourselves to cultivating our effects like opera singers. Let's see, what were you speaking about, exactly?

ROBESPIERRE. (*With the ghost of a smile*) The marriage of priests. I asked the Assembly to grant them permission to marry.

> MIRABEAU *eyes him sardonically.*

MIRABEAU. Most interesting. Of course, there wasn't any particular urgency—

ROBESPIERRE. (*Quietly*) I beg your pardon. There was urgency.

MIRABEAU. (*Bursts out laughing*) Do you think they're as frantic as all that? They can go on cuddling their housekeepers for a while yet. The Revolution has other fish to fry.

> He pats him kindly on the shoulder and takes out his snuffbox.

Believe me, young man, you didn't choose the subject of your first speech very well.

ROBESPIERRE. (*Insisting*) But I did, sir.

MIRABEAU. (*Offering him his snuffbox*) Do you take snuff?

ROBESPIERRE. No.

MIRABEAU. You should, it clears the mind. I can place you completely now. Maximilien de Robenpierre.

ROBESPIERRE. (*Correcting him*) Robespierre.

MIRABEAU. (*Not at all put out*) Robespierre. I like you very much. I know they laugh at you a bit, in the Assembly. Assemblies must always find themselves someone to laugh at, it eases tension. Try to arrange it so that this thankless role devolves on someone else. Better diction to begin with. There is also something a little dogmatic in you, a little pedantic, a little starchy, something—let's not mince words —a little boring which tends to put one off.

> He rises.

Having principles isn't enough, my dear boy. After all, we're in the theatre. You must learn the craft of the tragedian.

> He propels him gently toward the door.

Do come again, I shall always be glad to see you. And choose better subjects for your speeches.

ROBESPIERRE. (*Persistently*) Forgive me for persisting, sir. But I wanted to say that this proposal for the marriage of priests could please a large part of the minor clergy.

MIRABEAU. (*A little impatiently*) I don't doubt it. And I'll willingly discuss the matter with you some other time, but I am very busy today. (*He smiles and says with a certain amiable condescension*) I'll tell you a secret, I haven't had breakfast yet.

ROBESPIERRE. (*With a humble smirk*) I know it's very uncouth of me to cling on like this. I am uncouth. That's another reason why they laugh at me in the Assembly. I only wanted to say that strength, the strength we need, cannot be the achievement of a single man, even a man of genius like yourself. The minor clergy in France number some eighty thousand priests who are powerful electors. One can think what one likes of the urgency of their right to marry, but getting them married is the only way to bind them to the Revolution.

MIRABEAU. (*Who has already opened the door, turns and looks at him*) You are a queer fish. Is that what you wanted to say in the debate? Why on earth didn't you say it then?

ROBESPIERRE. (*Humbly*) I did. But I wasn't able to make myself heard. *I* haven't any genius, you see.

MIRABEAU. (*Studying him*) Where does strength lie then?

ROBESPIERRE. (*With a soft gleam in his eye*) In the second-rate, since they are the majority.

MIRABEAU. (*Heavily, after a pause*) I don't like the second-rate.

ROBESPIERRE. (*Still softly*) We need them. What we have to do will only be done by them.

MIRABEAU. (*Murmurs, musing*) For them, perhaps.

ROBESPIERRE. (*More softly still*) Why not?

MIRABEAU. Because they are too near to petty things.

ROBESPIERRE. Is that their fault?

MIRABEAU. No, but it's a fact. To give them power would be to risk having them lose their way in secondary problems. The man who governs must rise a little higher than that. And their lives have not accustomed them to heights.

ROBESPIERRE. (*With sudden harshness*) Yet it is those second-rate men who will make the Revolution, whether you and your kind like it or not.

> MIRABEAU *looks him up and down, surprised by this change of tone.*

MIRABEAU. Who gave you leave to use that tone to me, my little friend?

ROBESPIERRE. (*With a venomous hiss which suddenly transforms him*) I'm one of them.

MIRABEAU. (*Going to him, heavy-footed and, jovial, taking his arm*) All right then, you listen to me. I would rather go and live in Constantinople, with the Grand Turk, than see six hundred nonentities make or break France; declare themselves in power for life, perhaps, in the name of the few million nonentities who elected them.

ROBESPIERRE. (*Hissing*) And what if those few millions of nonentities are France?

MIRABEAU. (*Thundering*) They live in France. But it wasn't they who made it! Do you think France was built the way one runs a grocer's shop? The men who built France had nothing in common with them but the fact of having two arms and two legs, but, I regret to inform you, heads that towered over theirs!

ROBESPIERRE. (*Dropping the mask suddenly*) In the years that are coming, we shall have to get busy cutting off those towering heads. Might you be unaware of that, Comte Mirabeau?

MIRABEAU. (*With sudden anger*) Comte Mirabeau sends you to hell, you young pipsqueak, where he's been sending all the Mirabeau counts in his family ever since he reached the age of understanding. And he will not allow a little runt to pass judgment on him now! (*He controls his anger abruptly and goes on more calmly*) Get the devil out of here!

> *He takes his arm and calmly draws him to the door.* ROBESPIERRE *follows, resisting a little.*

Was it to treat me to drivel of this sort that you asked to see me?

ROBESPIERRE. (*Distorted with hate*) I came to see you because I admired you!

MIRABEAU. (*Cheerfully*) Well, that's one load less for you to carry then! Admiration is always heavy!

ROBESPIERRE. I hate you now.

MIRABEAU. (*Smiling*) Do. That may lend a little tone to your next speech. Cultivate your diction, young man, as well as your hates. And try to be likable. In France, one can do nothing without charm. Take that poor old Louis XVI, who hasn't any, look at the mess he's in.

ROBESPIERRE. (*Yelping*) I don't want to be charming! I'll never charm anybody!

MIRABEAU. No, I'm afraid you won't. I'll ring for someone to see you out.
He rings a bell.

ROBESPIERRE. (*Shouting, contorted with hatred*) I don't need your lackeys to show me to the door!
He spits on the floor.

MIRABEAU. (*Pained*) My dear boy. One can serve the Revolution and be polite as well.

ROBESPIERRE. (*Shouting*) No!

MIRABEAU. (*Shrugging*) To prove it to you, I shall see you to your carriage myself.

ROBESPIERRE. I haven't got a carriage!

MIRABEAU. (*Lightly, pushing him gently out*) Don't boast about it! It's a great inconvenience.

ROBESPIERRE. (*Clinging to the door, one doesn't quite know why*) I do boast about it!

MIRABEAU. (*Resignedly*) Very well.
He looks at him before he goes.

You've taught me a very sad thing, which is that the Revolution could be a bore. I thought it young and gay.

ROBESPIERRE. (*Shouting after him*) Frivolous! Frivolous, the lot of you! A witty phrase consoles you for everything. France will have to stop being frivolous one day—she'll have to become a bore like me before she's properly clean at last!

> *He brushes himself down in an abrupt, nervous gesture.* SAINT-JUST *has just come in, brilliant, airy, very much at ease. He sees* ROBESPIERRE.

SAINT-JUST. Brushing yourself down again?

> ROBESPIERRE *stops guiltily.* SAINT-JUST *sees the birch at* ROBESPIERRE's *feet and picks it up.*

Do you think this birch will help you stop those sinister children playing with everything they see? Have you thought over what we talked about yesterday?

ROBESPIERRE. Yes.

SAINT-JUST. Danton said last night at Vefours—true, he was with women, but Danton always is with women—he said that one day the Republic, once out of danger, could afford clemency and forgive its enemies. It's a mere phrase. But this one, after your speech last week urging the Assembly to greater severity, is downright provocation. Are you going to let it pass?

ROBESPIERRE. (*Averting his eyes*) Danton was my comrade in arms for a long time. . . . Camille is still my friend.

SAINT-JUST. (*Smiling*) Your friend? Have you read the latest number of the *Cordelier Gazette*? He holds you up to ridicule! Here. The ink's still wet.

> ROBESPIERRE *snatches the paper and starts to read. Then he shouts suddenly:*

ROBESPIERRE. He dared?

SAINT-JUST. (*Calmly*) Ah. That's roused you. I knew they'd have to wound your vanity as a man of letters to get at you at all.

ROBESPIERRE. (*Advancing on him, shouting*) Saint-Just, I shan't stand for this!

SAINT-JUST. (*Still calm and smiling*) God be praised! They're doomed this time.
> *A pause.*

ROBESPIERRE. (*Dully*) This is a horrible decision to make. True, I've never liked Danton. (*Shouting*) Danton is a hog, a stinking, rotting, posturing showman!

SAINT-JUST. Calm down. Save yourself for the rostrum. You'll evaporate your indignation.

ROBESPIERRE. But Camille is a child. Reckless, frivolous, depraved, yes—

SAINT-JUST. (*Softly*) One dies for far less than that these days. The puppy has a cruel bite. Shall I read you his article? It's amusing, as a matter of fact, and well written. He's not without talent.
> ROBESPIERRE *snatches the paper and tears it up.*

ROBESPIERRE. (*Shouting*) No!
> *He pauses a moment and then says dully:*
It may be too soon. We've only just struck at Hébert.

SAINT-JUST. Your reluctance does credit to your finer feelings, Robespierre. But we'll give way to sentiment later on, when we've cleaned up the world. Today, our duty lies elsewhere. Danton and Camille stand in the way. You know that as well as I do.
> *A pause.*

ROBESPIERRE. (*Dully*) You'll have to speak against them, I couldn't do it. Friendship is a sentiment you don't flout with impunity.
> *He brushes himself down nervously, as if driven by a tic.*

SAINT-JUST. (*Gently*) Don't keep brushing yourself like that. You're quite clean.
> *He pulls out his writing pad.*

Now. The main points of the indictment?

> ROBESPIERRE *avoids his eyes. Then he pulls a piece of paper abruptly from his pocket and hands it to him.*

ROBESPIERRE. Here. I drew them up a week ago.

SAINT-JUST (*Smiling*) You might have spared me the trouble of persuading you.

> *He shuts the notebook.*

We're supposed to be dining with Danton and Camille at Tallien's. Shall I cancel the engagement?

> *In the semidarkness, the dinner guests settle themselves at the table and start to light the candles.*

ROBESPIERRE. (*After a pause*) No. We will offer up this painful ordeal as a sacrifice to the nation.

> SAINT-JUST *bursts out laughing and says, as he moves nonchalantly toward the table:*

SAINT-JUST. You are a splendid character, Robespierre! I never tire of watching you at work. And that may well be the secret of why I stayed faithful to you until my death. . . . You amused me.

ROBESPIERRE. (*Between his teeth*) Take care, Saint-Just!

SAINT-JUST. Of what? One has only one head. I've been gambling with it in your company for years.

> *He gives a laugh, standing at the table, as the scene merges into the dinner party.*

> ROBESPIERRE *has taken off* BITOS' *overcoat and bowler hat. He walks primly toward the dinner table, where the others greet him mockingly, to the tune of "La Carmagnole."*

> Shoulder to shoulder
> We shall stand
> And never fear the enemy.
> Shoulder to shoulder
> We shall stand

And never fear the enemy.
Fight for the Motherland,
Brothers in Liberty.
Ring, ring the cannonade.
Death to the foe!
Death to the foe!
Ring, ring the cannonade.
Death to the foe!

> DANTON *suddenly stops laughing and singing with the others and looks at* ROBESPIERRE.

DANTON. (*Shouting*) My friends! There is a traitor in our midst! Robespierre isn't drinking. Robespierre must drink.

ROBESPIERRE. (*Elbowing him away*) I'm not thirsty.

DANTON. Oh? Not thirsty?
> *He gets up and raises his glass in an ironic toast.*
To the Republic, the One and Indivisible! You're trapped! Tomorrow it will be in all the papers. In letters this high. Leave it to Hébert. "Patriots' dinner. Robespierre refuses to toast the Republic!"

ROBESPIERRE. I have a stomachache. I've drunk too much already.

DANTON. Drink all the same, little priest. If you don't, I'll tell Hébert and he'll print it in his paper.

ROBESPIERRE. Hébert was arrested this evening.
> *A pause. The singing stops. They are suddenly a little sobered.* DANTON *turns to* SAINT-JUST.

DANTON. Is it true?

SAINT-JUST. (*Rocking on his chair*) What Robespierre says is always true.

DANTON. When was this decided? (*Thundering as he bangs on the table*) Why wasn't I told?

ROBESPIERRE. (*Coldly*) Where were you last night? We looked for you.

DANTON. (*Smiling, with an expansive gesture*) At the whore-house, yes, I know. I must tell you about it, little priest. I found an amazing girl at the Palais Royal. A freak . . . She's ugly as sin, but when you undress her—

ROBESPIERRE. (*Stiffly*) Keep your filth to yourself.

DANTON. Callipygian Venus! She'd fleeced some bigwig during the Old Regime and do you know where the hangman —who was a humorist—branded his royal lily?

ROBESPIERRE. (*On the verge of hysteria*) I order you—do you hear?—I order you to be quiet!

DANTON. (*Charmingly*) Why? Are you going to accuse me of being a royalist because of that? Mark you, if the Revolution had been really vigilant, it should have stamped a cap of liberty on the other cheek. I'm with you there. There's something undercover in the whole affair which you ought to look into, Robespierre. I suspect that bum of being a meeting place for aristocrats.

ROBESPIERRE. (*Yelping*) Danton, don't think you can mock everything forever!

DANTON. (*Charmingly, thrusting his face into* ROBESPIERRE's) What needles you most, tell me, the royal lily or the girl's arse?

CAMILLE. (*Asks suddenly*) Who demanded the indictment of Hébert?

SAINT-JUST. (*Softly*) I did. In full agreement with Robespierre and with the Committee's unanimous vote. We had to put a stop to the provocation of rabble rousers. The Committee has approved my list.

DANTON. (*Into his glass*) And who's on your list?

SAINT-JUST. Hébert, Chabot, Clootz, Hérault de Séchelles, all proven royalists.

DANTON. (*Flinging away his glass with a sudden roar*) Rabbit's piss! (*He chokes and bellows*) I know we have to kill off a few more and I loathe that bunch as much as you do. But those fellows? Royalists?

SAINT-JUST. (*Lightly*) Royalists, Danton! Who would have thought it, eh?

DANTON. Dear old Clootz too—a royalist? Saint-Just, you elegant little viper, until the end of time they'll never know exactly what you were—dandy, imp of mischief, or destroying angel—but one thing is certain, you were very intelligent and—

SAINT-JUST. (*Interrupting, coldly*) And because I am very intelligent I have contrived to put Clootz on a royalist list, and likewise, Hérault de Séchelles, your enemy. Oh, yes, and Fabre d'Eglantine, I nearly forgot! In his case it's even simpler, he's a thief.

DANTON. (*Yelling*) Séchelles is my enemy, but he's no royalist!

SAINT-JUST. (*Shrugging*) You're a child, Danton.

CAMILLE. (*Leaping up*) And Fabre is not a thief! (*Turning to him*) Robespierre!

ROBESPIERRE. Yes.

CAMILLE. You know that—you know Fabre never stole!

ROBESPIERRE. (*Inscrutably*) I know that the Committee has decided that Fabre has stolen funds.

CAMILLE. (*With an anguished cry*) Have we no right to be men any more?

ROBESPIERRE. (*Coldly*) What do you mean by that?

CAMILLE. That intelligence of ours, that reason which was going to reshape the world? Must we stifle all that now?

ROBESPIERRE. (*Trenchantly*) When the Committee of Public Safety has so decided, yes.

CAMILLE. When we stood up on our chairs and spoke to the people for the first time in the Palais Royal, we demanded that intelligence and reason should always prevail against tyranny. And that's why the people followed us.

ROBESPIERRE. (*Quietly*) We killed tyranny, don't forget that.

CAMILLE. We didn't kill it! Where's the difference between the arbitrary rule of royal ministers and that of a handful of men whom we've made more powerful than ever they were?

ROBESPIERRE. (*Calmly*) I'm amazed that you can't see the difference, Camille.

CAMILLE. (*Shouting*) No! I can't see it! I can't see it any more.

ROBESPIERRE. (*Dryly*) This deficiency of perception could ruin you if you weren't among friends. When the King's ministers made arbitrary decisions they did so for what they called reasons of state. When the Committee of Public Safety makes decisions which may seem arbitrary to you, it makes them for the good of the people. That's the difference.

CAMILLE. Words.

ROBESPIERRE. (*Tersely*) They will do for me.

CAMILLE. Tyranny is tyranny!

ROBESPIERRE. Must I teach you your catechism? There isn't a ten-year-old dunce in the national schools who can't recite it better than you. The tyranny of kings is a crime! The tyranny of the people is sacred. (*He calms down, and smiles*) You distress me, Camille.

CAMILLE. (*Quietly*) Robespierre, we are not on the rostrum now. I've pulled political wires, just as you have—

ROBESPIERRE. (*Equally quietly*) You watch your words, Camille.

CAMILLE. —But we're among ourselves now, friends around a dinner table for an evening's relaxation. Battle companions, too. (*He adds tonelessly*) And we're even closer, you and I. I was a junior, Maximilien, at school, and you were already in the seniors. But I admired you, I followed you everywhere, I loved you.

ROBESPIERRE. (*Coldly*) I loved you, too.

CAMILLE. (*With a sudden cry, going to him*) I still admire and love you, Robespierre. Shall I beg you on my knees? Don't stay shut in that prison of logic and severity where we can't reach you. It's the little boy you dazzled long ago with your intelligence and your courage who's asking you that now.

ROBESPIERRE. (*Pulling* CAMILLE *roughly to his feet*) Get up. This is a ridiculous scene. It's late, we must go home. (*He turns smiling to* TALLIEN *and* THERESA) My dear Tallien, it's been delightful. Citizeness Tallien really is a marvelous hostess. (*He smiles ambiguously*) One must say that for ex-aristocrats, they did know how to entertain.

THERESA. (*Smiling*) Is that a threat? Must I pack my little bundle this evening, Robespierre?

ROBESPIERRE. (*Kissing her hand*) Dear lady, I was merely paying you a compliment.

DANTON. (*With a roar of mirth*) Dear lady! He called her dear lady! And he kissed her hand! Versailles! We're back at Versailles! Oh, now I can die happy! I'll gladly die tomorrow!

SAINT-JUST (*Smiling and still nonchalant*) One should never say that, Danton.

DANTON. (*Going to* ROBESPIERRE *and making his comic little bows*) Kissing the ladies' hands! Maximilien, you old rogue! Red heels to his shoes and we never knew it!
> He gives him a hefty slap on the back. ROBES-
> PIERRE staggers.

ROBESPIERRE. Imbecile!

DANTON. (*Putting a friendly arm around his neck*) Well—it's Tallien's wine, dammit—I'm in an imbecilic mood. . . . God, how we've complicated things with these brains of ours . . . and things are simple, Max my boy, very simple. They obey laws as old as the world, and between ourselves, you and I won't ever change them. We can draw up constitutions until we're blue in the face! Take strength now, physical strength. An idea comes into my head. I take you under the armpits and I lift you up.

He does so.

Here you are, up in the air; it makes absolutely no sense at all! You're wriggling, you'd like to come down. Not a chance! You can't. Now *that's* a simple thing. *There's* the real inequality between men!

ROBESPIERRE. (*Wriggling absurdly up in the air and squealing*) Stop it! Stop it, you fool! Put me down!

DANTON. (*Bawling like a street vendor*) I'm putting you down! But now watch this! I grip you around the throat, so!

ROBESPIERRE. (*Choking*) Danton, stop it! You're choking me!

DANTON. (*Softly*) I know I'm choking you.

He looks at the choking ROBESPIERRE.

How simple history could be, when you stop to think. But I don't want to deprive us all of Robespierre, friends. We should miss him.

He lets him go.

Simpler still. The arm. Just the arm!

He twists ROBESPIERRE'*s arm behind his back.*

I twist it very gently.

ROBESPIERRE. (*Sweating in his efforts not to cry out*) Stop it!

DANTON. (*Softly*) I'll bet you that in three seconds you're going to say you're sorry, Robespierre. Sorry for everything. Sorry for the past, for the future, for whatever I say. Nobody's a stoic when someone has hold of your arm like this.

ROBESPIERRE *grimaces with clenched teeth, and slithers to the floor.*

My friends, I am master of France! Say you're sorry, Robespierre. Say sorry, Robespierre. Say sorry. Come on, say sorry.

ROBESPIERRE. (*Writhing with pain*) Saint-Just . . . !

SAINT-JUST *has risen. Coldly he touches* DANTON
on the shoulder with his cane.

SAINT-JUST. Danton, I know you're drunk, but squeeze him
around the throat again and finish him off, or else stop it.
A game half-played is dangerous. . . .

DANTON. (*Smiling as he releases* ROBESPIERRE) No. It was
only for a little fun, between friends. I couldn't even kill
a chicken now. I have a horror of death.

> SAINT-JUST *smiles maliciously as* ROBESPIERRE
> *nervously brushes himself down.*

SAINT-JUST. You're getting old, Danton.

DANTON. (*Turning suddenly, says gravely*) Yes, Saint-Just, I'm
getting old. Blood is slowly beginning to turn my stomach.
And other things, tiny little everyday things which I didn't
even know existed, are starting to matter to me now.

SAINT-JUST. What things—may one know?

DANTON. Work, children, the sweets of friendship and love.
Everything that has always made men what they are until
now.

SAINT-JUST. (*Coldly*) In short, a complete counterrevolution-
ary program.

> He turns to ROBESPIERRE *with a smile.*

My dear Max, we're being very hard on them both. I can
quite see now why they are all for leniency.

> He nods his head ironically at CAMILLE *who is*
> *holding* LUCILE *close.*

Why cut off their heads just because they don't think our
way any more? All we have to do is pull a cotton nightcap
over them. Eh, Danton?

> He slaps DANTON *on the back. They both laugh.*

DANTON. Pending which, shall I drive you back to Paris, Max,
my lad?

ROBESPIERRE. (*Still brushing himself nervously*) There's no
other carriage!

SAINT-JUST. (*Softly, from behind him*) You're clean, stop brushing yourself.

TALLIEN. (*Smiling as if nothing much had happened and picking up a candle to see them out*) Camille, dear boy, you're young and generous hearted. But you'll learn when you grow up that those are no virtues for a public man. . . . I knew about the Committee's decision and tonight's arrests, but I didn't say a word during your argument, did you notice? We all know, and Robespierre best of all, that those men were not quite as black as we have to say they were. But we have to say so. The people need to have things spelled out for them. . . . Well, there it is. Those men will have been soldiers sacrificed on a field of battle, lost children of the Revolution. . . . Having obtained the required result, Robespierre himself will make it a point of honor—won't you, Robespierre?—to rehabilitate them one day.

ROBESPIERRE. Every drop of blood I'm forced to shed is wrung from my own veins, I promise you. But there is no friend I would not sacrifice to my duty, I can promise you that too.

TALLIEN. (*Smiling and putting a hand on* CAMILLE's *shoulder*) You understand, Camille?

CAMILLE. (*As if lost*) No, I don't. I don't understand anything any more. Let's go home, Lucile, I'm tired.

TALLIEN. (*Motioning to* THERESA) We'll see you to your carriage. . . .

THERESA. (*Going out on* DANTON's *arm*) Wonderful night for April, isn't it?

TALLIEN. (*Softly, as he goes out*) Floreal, beloved, Floreal, not April. You'll have to remember the new names, my darling, or you'll get us into trouble. (*He sighs*) Poor Fabre! All there'll be left of him is a calendar and a song. Do you remember, my love, "Il pleut il pleut, Bergère" . . . Charming little thing. . . .

He goes out humming. ROBESPIERRE *has hung back a little.* LUCILE *comes back into the room suddenly and stops just outside the circle of light. He has stopped too.*

LUCILE. (*Quietly*) You can't have Camille killed, Robespierre.

ROBESPIERRE. (*Stiffly, with a faint hint of falseness in his tone*) I would sacrifice myself if necessary. Greatness is very costly.

LUCILE. (*Looking at him*) What is greatness?

ROBESPIERRE. The ruthless fulfillment of one's duty.

LUCILE. (*Still quietly*) And what is your duty?

ROBESPIERRE. To follow a straight road whatever the cost, right to that clearing in the forest where the Revolution will at last be complete.

LUCILE. What if that clearing receded as it does in fairy tales?

ROBESPIERRE. Then we should have to continue the struggle.

LUCILE. Forever?

ROBESPIERRE. Forever.

LUCILE. Without concern for people?

ROBESPIERRE. Without concern for people.

LUCILE. (*Still softly*) But it's for people that you want this Revolution.

ROBESPIERRE. (*Brushing a thought away with his hand*) For other people, without faces.
    A pause.

LUCILE. (*Gently*) Robespierre. I'm only a woman. But women know things that you don't know. Life is made in the depths of their wombs. They have known since always that, in the daytime, there are no men. You've all of you stayed little boys, with your ideas, your assurance which nothing can shake, your fits of violence. . . .

ROBESPIERRE. (*With an impatient gesture*) Excuse me, Lucile, but I have important business. . . .

LUCILE. (*Smiling*) Of course! Right from the age of fifteen, you've all had so many things to do, always! Becoming generals, discovering the North Pole, getting rich, building the reign of Justice, taking your revenge. . . . Your plans haven't changed since your voices broke. And not one of you set yourself the task of just becoming a man.

ROBESPIERRE. (*With another impatient gesture*) Lucile—

LUCILE. Everything you've just said to me I've heard Camille say, almost to a word. I used to smile and run my fingers through his hair, and I'd go and cook his supper, so that he'd at least eat something. Then the night came and he'd fall asleep at last, defeated, in the hollow of my arm, a man again. I didn't sleep. I looked at my man as he slept, savoring the weight of his head on my shoulder, of his leg across my body. I weighed his real weight as a man, at last, as all silent women do at night.

> *A short pause. She asks gently.*

Nobody has ever watched you sleeping, have they, Robespierre?

ROBESPIERRE. (*Stiffly*) No.

LUCILE. They'll feel the want of that, when they come to weigh up exactly what you were.

ROBESPIERRE. (*With a sudden cry*) Nobody will ever need to know who I was. I was nothing.

> *He brushes himself down. Another pause.* LU-
> CILE *says very quietly:*

LUCILE. Give me back Camille's weight on my shoulder, Robespierre. Not because he was your friend at school— boys of fifteen are intoxicated with the thought of sacrificing their best friends to a cause. Give him back to me because you loved me once.

> *A pause.*

ROBESPIERRE. (*Stiffly*) If I did that, I should be a coward.

LUCILE. (*Scarcely audibly*) What is a coward? Past the age of fifteen, nobody knows that either.

Another pause. She murmurs wearily:
Very well. I shall go and join Camille alone, since you
won't give him back to me.
*She moves away gently, already a shadow. On
the edge of the circle of light she turns and says:*
Poor Robespierre, who kills because he couldn't succeed
in growing up. . . .
She has gone. ROBESPIERRE *is alone in the middle
of the stage, stiff and tense. A spasm distorts
his face and he murmurs:*

ROBESPIERRE. No, I haven't grown up. I still hate people.
Big fat Mirabeau, with his potbelly and his smile; taking
my arm with his stubby ringed fingers and trying to throw
me out. (*He rubs his arm*) And the Jesuit father with his
birch. "Do you know why you are going to be whipped,
Robespierre?" And Danton with his big voice and his man's
smell. "Say sorry, Robespierre! Say sorry, Robespierre.
Say sorry."
*He breaks into sudden, hysterical laughter and
yelps.*
Say sorry, Danton!
*He brushes something off his lapel, straightens
his clothes and goes on composedly.*
I'll teach them to frighten me. That big Samson who chops
their heads off, he stinks too, him and his two assistants with
their brawny arms. And they smile fatly at the girls from
the top of the scaffold because they know that the bitches
will be waiting for them at night, warm and damp and
willing. (*He hisses*) Whores! Wait though, my pretties.
Those hefty lovers, those strong-limbed bulls, those males
of yours—you don't know that Robespierre, little Robespierre, has only to look at them, Robespierre who's so thin
and ugly.
*He glares with malicious irony and then rocks
with mirth.*
Why, what's come over them? Have their big arms lost
their power suddenly? Has that thing, that hideous thing

that strains their breeches, disappeared? Turn around, ladies! Whatever can it be? Another even stronger male? An even bigger, brawnier bull? No. It's just little Robespierre is looking at them. Like this!

> *He stares at an imaginary male, then gives a short cackle and spits.*

Whores! I'll show you. I'll widow the lot of you!

> *He puts on Bitos' hat and coat. He starts to brush himself down frantically, with a satisfied snigger.* SAINT-JUST *comes in.*

SAINT-JUST. You must stop brushing yourself down like that. It's a ridiculous habit. What were you doing all alone in this empty room? Rehearsing your speech?

> ROBESPIERRE *goes to him, panting. This whole scene is played in a tempo of fevered inspiration.*

ROBESPIERRE. Saint-Just, there is in this race of people an incurable bent for fecklessness and easy living. They're more interested in playing bowls or fondling girls than carving out their destiny. I used to loathe the aristocrats, but the lowest laborer in France still wears red satin heels. Insolent nation!

SAINT-JUST. (*Smiling*) Do you want to pass a law against insolence?

ROBESPIERRE. I want to pass a law forcing them to relearn the meaning of respect.

> *He sidles over to him.*

We must re-create their God for them. A God of our own making. A God whom we'll keep well under control. A decree, that's all we want. Article One. The people of France acknowledge the existence of the Supreme Being. Article Two: They acknowledge that the worship of the Supreme Being is the guiding beacon of man's duties.

SAINT-JUST. (*Straight-faced*) Are you sure that means anything?

ROBESPIERRE. (*Unaware of the irony*) Yes. Article Three: All blasphemers will be punished by death.

SAINT-JUST. (*Laughing*) Well, that means something anyhow! (*He goes on*) Make a decree, work your guillotine. They'll cheat your God, whatever name you give Him. They all cheat. It's in their blood.

ROBESPIERRE. (*Shouting*) I'll kill them if they cheat! Do I cheat? I'll kill every single one who cheats! I'll guillotine everybody! And I'll rebuild the country—afterwards. Tomorrow I'll pass a law reforming the Revolutionary Tribunal. It's all too slow! What we lack is the instrument. You write it down. Article One: The Revolutionary Tribunal is set up to punish the enemies of the people. Article Two: The enemies of the people are those who try to annihilate liberty—

SAINT-JUST. (*Jotting it down in his notebook*) Liberty.
> *He glances up at* ROBESPIERRE *who is looking at him.*

ROBESPIERRE. (*Goes on, unheedingly*)—Article Three: The penalty laid down for all offenses is death.

SAINT-JUST. (*Writing it down*) Death.

ROBESPIERRE. (*In full creative euphoria*) Article Four: If proof exists, no witnesses will be brought. Article Five: The defense of traitors is classed as conspiracy. The law gives patriots the defense of patriotic juries. It grants none to conspirators!
> *He drops into a chair, exhausted by his shouting, and brushes himself down.* SAINT-JUST *calmly reads over his notes.*

SAINT-JUST. To take effect retrospectively. Prejudiced juries. No defense. It's a model of its kind. It will be used again. (*He asks*) Who will arraign for the Tribunal?

ROBESPIERRE. The Committee of Public Safety.

SAINT-JUST. Who will provide the Committee with names?

ROBESPIERRE. A Commission, unknown to the Committee, will draw up lists of suspects. The Committee will merely sign them and hand them on to the Tribunal.

SAINT-JUST. And the Tribunal?

ROBESPIERRE. The Tribunal will pass sentence.

SAINT-JUST. (*A little taken aback, even so*) But then who will have tried them?

ROBESPIERRE. (*Mysteriously, as if soothed*) Nobody. The machinery of the law. We must install reliable nobodies, interlock them like cogs in a machine, and dispense as far as possible with the human element, so that everything will seem to decide itself. I myself shall withdraw. The wheels of the law will grind alone.
> *He brushes himself.*

SAINT-JUST. (*Smiling, as he pockets his notebook*) Stop brushing yourself. And where does God come into this? Have you forgotten Him?
> ROBESPIERRE *stops brushing and stands up, relaxed and calm.*

ROBESPIERRE. No. We'll start with God. We must give the people back a moral sense. Besides, they need a holiday to help them forget Danton. This evening I shall read the decree on the Supreme Being. I want a celebration, a very fine, very touching celebration. We'll remove the guillotine—just for one day. I want flowers, lots of flowers, girls in white dresses, children—oh, the innocence of children!—choral singers. Something which will uplift us all! I can't do everything!
> *Blackout suddenly. When the lights go up again,* CHARLES *is by the table, in ordinary clothes, holding a basin. Everyone crowds around* BITOS, *who is squatting on the floor, nursing his chin. Outside, a heavy rainstorm can be heard.*

BITOS. (*Holding his jaw, says venomously*) I shall prefer a charge! Attempted murder. Article 117.

MAXIME. (*Smiling*) No, no, Bitos. You just fainted with
fright. The gun wasn't loaded. Robespierre was shot in
the jaw. But not you. I put a little too much powder in,
that's all. Give him the glass, Charles, and let him see for
himself.

> CHARLES *hands the mirror to* BITOS, *who slowly
> and suspiciously lets go of his chin. He looks so
> funny as he tests the state of his jaw that the
> others can contain themselves no longer and
> burst out laughing. He leaps to his feet, shout-
> ing.*

BITOS. My hat! And my coat!

> CHARLES *hands him his little overcoat and his
> bowler. Outside one hears the thunder and the
> rain falling in sheets.* BITOS *gravely puts on his
> hat after a sort of collective bow and says shortly:*

Thank you.

PHILIPPE. (*Stepping forward*) You really ought to let Verdreuil and me drive you home. You can't go out in this
rain in white stockings and pumps.

BITOS. (*Vexed, going up the stairs*) I shall find a taxi.

MAXIME. (*Shouting up at him*) At midnight, in a provincial
town, nobody has ever found a taxi, Bitos.

> CHARLES *steps forward and says to* BITOS, *who is
> hovering on the threshold, battling with the
> door against the wind:*

CHARLES. Perhaps I could lend you my umbrella, sir.

BITOS. Thank you.

> *He takes the umbrella and tries vainly to open it
> against the wind.*

CHARLES. (*Crying out anxiously*) It's a little stiff. If you'll
allow me, sir?

BITOS. (*With a jaundiced smile*) Robespierre may not have

known how to boil an egg, but I am still capable of opening an umbrella!

He lunges into the wind.

CHARLES. (*Increasingly worried, cries*) Careful, sir, please! You have to know the way of it. It's a little nervy, is that umbrella.

> BITOS *has forced open the umbrella, determined at all costs to get the better of it. The thing is now inside out.*

CHARLES. There! I knew it! You have to know how to handle it. It's very sensitive.

> BITOS *throws the umbrella at him with a baleful look and clutching his hat with both hands hurls himself into the storm amid the general laughter, not without the door bashing into his face first.*

A WOMAN'S VOICE. The door! Shut the door!

> MAXIME *starts to run up the stairs.* VULTURNE *follows him up.*

VULTURNE. (*Yelling against the wind and the growling storm*) Maxime! We've got to bring him back! If you let him leave like this, tomorrow he'll bring a charge and young Delanoue will go back to jail.

> MAXIME *looks at him, then snatches off his wig, turns his collar up and starts after* BITOS. BRASSAC, *who has done likewise, joins him.*

BRASSAC. No! Not you, Maxime. I employ twenty thousand factory hands. Pacifying the people is my job. Your gamp, Charles!

> CHARLES, *who has mended it, hands him the umbrella.* BRASSAC *seizes it and dashes out, shouting over his shoulder.*

I'll bring him back. You'll have to flatter him. Lila, I'm counting on you. Don't forget, Bitos is a snob at heart and he particularly values the good opinion of the class he's intending to have shot one day.

He vanishes into the night.

MAXIME. (*Turning to* CHARLES) Charles, bring us some whisky.

CHARLES. (*Pained*) Between courses, sir?

MAXIME. (*Firmly*) Between courses, Charles.
> CHARLES *goes out with a disillusioned shrug.*

CURTAIN

ACT THREE

Everyone is onstage, waiting anxiously. BRASSAC
*pokes his head in through the kitchen door. He
has shed his wig. He is wearing a blanket over
his shoulders and is wiping his hair dry with a
towel.*

BRASSAC. He's telephoning for a friend to come and fetch him
in his car, but I've persuaded him to come in and get warm.
He's soaked to the skin. He's afraid of pneumonia, that's
really why he came back. He fusses terribly about his health.
He vanishes again like a jack-in-the-box. DES-
CHAMPS, *who has been standing a little apart
from the others, now steps forward.*

DESCHAMPS. I see you're very wisely trying to smooth things
over with Bitos. As my being here certainly wouldn't help,
I must ask you to let me leave.

MAXIME. (*With a smile*) Yes. One can sometimes make it up
with one's class enemies, even after a bloodbath, but never
with one's friends.
He rings. CHARLES *appears.*
Charles, M. Deschamps' coat, please.

DESCHAMPS. But before I go I would like to say that I share
André Bitos' political ideas even if I despise him as a man.

MAXIME. I did realize that.

DESCHAMPS. That's what prevented me from doing honor to
your invitation. I haven't been a very entertaining guest.
I'm sorry.
He puts on the raincoat which CHARLES *brings
him.*

I hope this evening will end for the best, for all of you. Good night, sir. I'm very happy to have met you.

> *He takes a step, then turns with a shy delightful smile.*

By all means tame "the people," as M. Brassac calls them —with methods which I would rather not witness. . . . What I would like to tell you is that neither André Bitos, nor the ringleaders of M. Brassac's factories, nor, incidentally, those figures of the Revolution we tried to bring to life this evening, are the people. All those men are more like yourselves than you can possibly imagine. The people, the real people, have the distinction and the elegance to belong to the race that does nothing else but give. (*He smiles again*) That's a bit high-sounding, I apologize, but I didn't quite know how to say this to you and I did want to say it. . . . Enjoy your evening, ladies, what remains of it.

VICTOIRE. I should like to leave too, Maxime. I'm sure M. Deschamps would see me home.

MAXIME. My angel, the main thing now is to prevent young Delanoue from footing the bill. You women will have your work cut out, all three of you. (*To* DESCHAMPS *who stands waiting*) I'll see you out.

LILA. (*To the others as she watches* DESCHAMPS *go*) He's extremely nice, that young man. Not invitable, but very nice.

AMANDA. (*Ruefully*) Oh dear, why did he let him leave? He had the most divine eyes.

> BRASSAC *comes in with* BITOS, *who is now without his wig, his hair wet, a towel around his neck and a sort of absurd curtain over his shoulders which gives him a vaguely Roman look.*

BRASSAC. Friends, very sportingly, I must say, Bitos accepts our apologies and has agreed to come and have a drink with us. What a filthy night. We're drenched to the bone.

BITOS. (*Still on his guard*) I was anxious to show these ladies that I wasn't as much of a bear as they say. I lost my temper for a second, quite justifiably, as I'm sure you'll agree— and I should like to apologize myself.

LILA. M. Bitos, I knew you had a sense of humor.
> MAXIME *comes forward, bottle in hand.*

MAXIME. Here, Bitos, in token of our reconciliation.

BITOS. (*With a prudent gesture*) A drop, just a drop.

MAXIME. (*Pouring him a drink*) Drink up.
> *He rubs him down.*

Are you feeling warmer now? Your friend Deschamps sent his apologies, he had to leave. I thought it best not to try to keep him here. He struck me as curiously hostile toward you.

BITOS. He *is* hostile. (*He drinks and coughs*) You've made this too strong. Yes, it's a fact, that young man is among the many who cannot forgive me for my success. . . .

MAXIME. (*Giving him a final rub*) What a very ugly sentiment.

BITOS. It's very difficult to rise above certain mediocre individuals and still keep their good will.

MAXIME. You know the human heart, I see.
> *He exchanges a look with the others and then goes on pouring drinks for all the people grouped around Bitos.*

Personally, I had no idea there had been any trouble between you. Over young Delanoue I must plead guilty. I yielded to a certain taste for cheap theatricals in getting him to come here. But I never thought he would indulge in such a dubious piece of foolery. We do all agree, don't we—it was only foolery?

BITOS. (*Woodenly*) We'll say no more about it. This is entirely my affair.

VULTURNE. (*Rather too cordially*) Bitos is right! After all, there's no harm done, is there? I behaved none too pleasantly myself. I apologize. Do you know, I swear I thought I was Mirabeau and in the heat of the moment—

BITOS. (*With an enigmatic smile*) Why not? I certainly thought I was Robespierre.

MAXIME. (*Filling his glass*) Drink up, friends, and let's forget it.

AMANDA *fills* BITOS' *glass. He protests laughingly.*

BITOS. Ho, ho there! Steady! You'll make me drunk.

AMANDA. (*Murmuring in his ear*) I should adore that! You're such a mysterious person, André.

BITOS. (*Purring, very much the man of the world*) I assure you there's nothing mysterious about me. One can be a "red," as you call it, and still enjoy a little pleasant relaxation. I've appeared at a few fashionable social gatherings.

He is sitting center stage in an armchair into which JULIEN *has pushed him, holding court suddenly, with the women fluttering around him, while the men crowd around filling his glass.* LILA *draws up a stool beside him.*

LILA. My dear André, it's just this blend of progressive thought and impeccable behavior which makes you such a welcome guest.

BITOS. (*Bowing*) Thank you.

LILA. Are you free on Wednesday week? I'm having a few people to dinner.

BITOS. (*Pleasantly surprised, while* MAXIME *takes the opportunity of filling his glass*) I should be delighted to be among your guests on this occasion.

He drains his glass euphorically and coughs.

My friend will be arriving soon. I woke him in the middle of the night, poor fellow, and he'll need time to dress.

A pause. The rain is heard. BITOS *adds, by way of apology:*

But this weather isn't fit for a dog to go out in. And as I'm a little chesty . . .

> BRASSAC *makes a sign to* LILA *who says quickly:*

LILA. We'll be really sorry to sit down to dinner again without you. Couldn't we telephone to tell him not to bother?

BITOS. No, he's sure to be on his way by now.

LILA. Then why don't we ask him to join us?

AMANDA. (*Taking his arm*) What a good idea! I should so love you to stay.

BITOS. (*With a little embarrassed laugh*) Well, he's a very nice young fellow, extremely worthy really . . . but very ordinary. He's the garage man from the market square.

JULIEN. Fessard? Why, I know him like the back of my hand! Which reminds me, I haven't paid him for my car yet.

BITOS. (*With a forced smile*) And as a good tradesman he's bound to have far stricter notions about debt than men of your social set, so—

BRASSAC. (*Very cordially*) My dear Bitos, the thing that delights me about you is your ability to mix. You tell us that Fessard is a friend of yours, and yet one meets you at Lila's dinner parties, which are the most exclusive in the neighborhood. You're an amazing man.

MAXIME. (*Filling everyone's glass*) You're not drinking, friends, you're not drinking.

> BITOS, *his glass filled despite his halfhearted protest, goes on very animatedly.*

BITOS. Why amazing? There are goodhearted, interesting people everywhere. I personally make no distinction between a mechanic like Fessard—provided he's not stupid—and a guest at a smart function.

JULIEN. Who isn't necessarily stupid either!

BITOS. (*Laughing with lordly geniality*) Not necessarily!

BRASSAC. (*Taking the bottle and refilling his glass as he says with a sigh*) Oh, Bitos . . . We really should get to know each other better. Why this totally false reputation for being a puritan? Do you foster it yourself? Why, you're a very good drinker!

BITOS. (*Flattered*) Oh, in moderation.
>> *He drinks and then coughs atrociously.*

BRASSAC. They say that you're afraid of women, too. But I saw you at Clermont once, in most voluptuous company.

BITOS. (*With an inane delighted laugh*) You may have seen me with a lady, I don't say that isn't quite possible, but in most voluptuous company, as you put it—well . . .

BRASSAC. Enough said, Bitos! As one gay dog to another! No need to explain!
>> *He winks and digs him in the ribs.*
Anyway, she was a very attractive redhead.

MAXIME. (*Exclaiming*) Lea! My dear Bitos, congratulations. She's the most expensive girl in town.

JULIEN. (*Patting him on the back*) Lea? Don't tell me the dear creature is playing me false? Are we going to have to fight over her? Bitos, you old scoundrel you!
>> *The three men crowd around him, slapping him on the back.* BITOS *drinks, coughs and splutters, in seventh heaven.* JULIEN *tries to refill his glass.* BITOS *refuses. The bottle goes round behind him and comes back to* AMANDA.

BITOS. Gentlemen, gentlemen! I thought one of the rules of your world was discretion over these little . . . escapades— if only out of regard for the ladies.

BRASSAC. Gentlemen, Bitos is reminding us of our manners and he's right.

AMANDA. (*Refilling* BITOS' *glass from the other side*) A little more whisky?

BITOS. (*Blossoming imperceptibly*) I won't say no . . . Most agreeable, it has quite a smoky taste.

BRASSAC. Whisky's the most innocuous drink in the world.

MAXIME. Charles, bring another bottle!

BRASSAC. It's made from cereals, did you know? And what could be more wholesome than cereals? More socially meaningful? Barley, rye . . .

MAXIME. Wheat.

JULIEN. Collective farms!

BRASSAC. Our daily bread! Brandy, wine, that's suspect. It's the grape. And the grape is Bacchus. And who says Bacchus says Dionysius. And who says Dionysius is already a counter-revolutionary!

BITOS. (*Amused, says subtly*) I never suspected all this culture, Brassac. But why the devil should Dionysius be a counter-revolutionary?

BRASSAC. Because Dionysius is anarchy. And I'm sure I needn't tell you that when revolutionaries seize power, the first people they shoot are invariably the anarchists. Dammit, you wouldn't want those hysterical maniacs stirring up a whole lot of strikes, would you? Especially when it's the people who govern.

BITOS. (*Suddenly conspiratorial, raising his glass and drinking with him*) I see there's a lot in the running of this world that hasn't escaped your notice, my dear Brassac.

BRASSAC. (*Following suit*) Ah, my dear Bitos, one knows instantly, with certain men, that there's everything to be gained by being frank. Intelligence is an Internationale too, let's not forget that.

BITOS. (*Beaming and raising his glass*) Allow me to return the compliment, my dear fellow.

BRASSAC. (*Confidentially*) They're always harping on your massacres, but do you think our side ever held our horses, eh?

A wink and a dig in the ribs. BITOS *giggles and follows suit.*

BITOS. (*Delightedly*) So you've admitted it, at last!

BRASSAC. (*Winking and putting a finger to his lips*) Shush! Officially one never admits anything.

BITOS. (*Sniggering conspiratorially*) You said it, I didn't. But then, why blame us, at the Liberation?

BRASSAC. (*Confidentially*) But we don't! We don't blame you for anything at all! We aren't children! Summary executions are the French national game.

BITOS. (*Captious suddenly, in his drink*) Ah, no. No, no. There you're wrong. We always took care—in '93 I'm talking about—to see that the decisions of the Revolutionary Tribunal were perfectly in order. Always two signatures.

BRASSAC. But so do we, my dear man, so do we! We aren't savages! Two, three signatures, four if necessary! In France you can always find a general to sign a decree or turn down a reprieve, and if there isn't the right law to hand, you pass one, with retroactive effect, naturally! We know the form. We kill, yes, but we do it in the proper manner. In France we dine off severed heads. It's the national dish.

BITOS. (*With an unlovely little gesture*) The iron fist! That's the whole secret. And no need for the velvet glove either. But wait!

> *He lifts a drunken, warning finger and adds thickly:*

For the good of the people!

JULIEN. (*Softly, behind him*) And who decides what's the good of the people?

BITOS. (*Innocently*) We do!

> *He says this so seriously that their control breaks and they all burst out laughing. He looks at them, a little put out, then suddenly joins in the laughter. Under cover of it, his glass is filled again.*

JULIEN. (*Slapping him on the back*) Good old Bitos! I like him now.

LILA. (*Tweaking his ear and laughing*) And he's so clever!

BITOS. (*Gurgling ludicrously*) You're too kind!

BRASSAC. (*Raising his glass*) Gentlemen, Robespierre! A little more whisky, Bitos, to drink Robespierre's health.

BITOS. Delighted, thank you! I've quite grown to like it now!

AMANDA. Neat! And bottoms up!

BITOS. (*The gay dog. He cries in his squeaky voice*) Bottoms up! To Robespierre, gentlemen!

ALL. (*Raising their glasses*) To Robespierre!
> BITOS *drains his glass at one gulp and coughs horribly.*

VULTURNE. (*Moving to* MAXIME) Stop the game now, Maxime, it's going to turn ugly.
> MAXIME *has been sitting silently in a corner, pale and malicious.*

MAXIME. You're mad! I've never seen anything so marvelous.

PHILIPPE. (*Moving to him*) We must get him to agree not to prosecute young Delanoue now, while he's still drunk.
> VULTURNE *exchanges a look with* PHILIPPE *and goes to* BITOS.

VULTURNE. My dear Bitos, I should like to ask you a favor—

BITOS. (*Suspicious suddenly*) Yes? What's that?

VULTURNE. It's about that boy—whom Maxime should never have brought into his lunatic charade in the first place. Any charge brought against him now could get him into serious trouble, as you know—

BITOS. (*Interrupting, suddenly deadly serious*) M. de Verdreuil, I have every regard for you, but I've told you already, this is entirely my concern. The dignity of my robes is at stake.

AMANDA. (*Winningly*) To please me. I promise you a little reward if you agree not to get that poor boy into trouble.

LILA. It will cause a tremendous stir, you can count on me for that. Just think, a prosecuting counsel dropping a charge! (*She turns to him*) Besides, pardons are all the rage now, have you noticed?
> *A pause. Everyone looks at* BITOS *as he sits there, embarrassed by the women's caresses. He hiccups with drunken gravity.*

BITOS. (*More and more the great Caesar, draped in his curtain*) Very well. As the ladies all wish it, I incline toward clemency.

ALL. Long live Bitos! Here's to Bitos!
> *They all drink to him.*

MAXIME. Do we have your word, Bitos?

BITOS. (*Noble and drunk*) You do. I shouldn't be doing this, of course. Clemency toward the enemies of the people is a crime. But tonight's a special occasion. We can stretch a principle or two.
> *Holding out his glass.*

Give me another whisky.
> *The three men all rush forward with three bottles. Everyone laughs.*

AMANDA. Thank you. My turn to pay now. There. (*She kisses him*) You're very very kind.

BITOS. (*Bewildered, nervously wiping his lipstick-stained mouth and exclaiming with sudden truculence*) Yes, I am! I'm very kind indeed. Nobody believes I'm a kind man. They hate me!

AMANDA. (*Cajoling him*). No, they don't. They admire you and like you—everybody does!

BITOS. I was accused of being harsh after the Liberation. But we had to sweep up the mess. France wasn't clean. You want France to be clean, don't you?

EVERYBODY. (*Playing up to him, soothing him and sitting him down again*) Of course we do, M. Bitos, of course we do! Now, you mustn't worry! France is quite clean.

BITOS. (*Suddenly voluble, a mass of nervous tics*) It's like that fellow Lucien, the one that rat Deschamps told you about. Do you think it didn't cost me a great deal to demand his death? I made my first communion with him!

EVERYBODY. (*Soothingly*) Of course it did, Bitos! Of course! It must have cost you a great deal. We understand.

BITOS. Do you think it's funny having to go out at dawn and watch somebody you know being put to death? It's horrible!

AMANDA. (*Caressing him*) Poor Bitos . . .

BITOS. (*Shouting*) I bought a doll for his little girl! The most expensive doll I could find! So why do people say I'm not kind?

AMANDA. Yes, why do they? It's not fair.

BITOS. (*Sitting up straight*) No, it *isn't* fair! Everybody's unfair to me, all the time! And it hurts. (*He shouts suddenly*) Everything hurts me!

> To VICTOIRE, *who is sitting in a corner, pale and silent.*

Mlle. de Brèmes, your father drove me out like a beggar because I dared to ask for your hand!

> To LILA.

And you, madame, at that dinner party you invited me to last winter, you saw what I'd done, you saw that I'd used the wrong fork! Anyway, your butler saw it! And nobody warned me! They let me go right on, using the wrong things, until when the meat arrived all I had left was my pastry fork! They wanted me to look ridiculous! You, Maxime, it's true I used to carry your books on our school walks so you could run about. It's true I made myself your valet, it's true I loved you. But you repulsed me. Everybody always repulses me. And yet I'm a kind man! I'm kind! I'm kind!

He shouts like a madman.

I wouldn't harm a fly!

He is somber and crushed. Suddenly he hiccups and drops into a chair which someone has charitably placed under his behind. He says suddenly in a strange voice:

It wasn't my fault I was poor. You never took anything seriously, and yet you succeeded in everything you did, always. (*He adds dully*) The world of the poor collapses if people don't take things seriously. It's like a blow in the face.

There is a sort of embarrassment, even in those who were openly enjoying it all a moment before. VULTURNE *looks at* PHILIPPE. *They go to* BITOS.

PHILIPPE. M. Bitos, it's late and you're tired. Wouldn't you like us to drive you home?

He gets up.

MAXIME. (*Catching him up*) Bitos, you've just upset me very much. I thought we were friends again.

BITOS. (*Looking at him coldly*) No, I have no friends. I don't love anybody. Not even the people. (*He looks at them strangely and says*) The iron fist.

A pause. He adds maliciously:

That's my only love.

He brushes himself, dazed. Suddenly he becomes aware of them all, standing silent and a little afraid around him. He breaks into a laugh and says softly:

Well, well! Little Bitos who was so comical just now, eh? Not laughing now, are we?

The others stand there, dumb-struck. Only BRASSAC *recovers his composure and goes to him, gravely friendly.*

BRASSAC. Bitos, this evening's regrettable adventure has at least accomplished something. It's taught us what you are. If France is to rise again, it won't be through systems but through men. Unfortunately men are rare.

BITOS. (*Contemptuously*) Yes, men are rare.

BRASSAC. (*Sententiously*) You'll forgive my frankness, but I'm not altogether sure that the political forces which employ you are precisely aware of your true worth. (*Slyly pouring* BITOS *a drink*) You know that I belong to what is sometimes called "Progressive Management." There are a few big employers of labor like myself who put the social question before everything else. Your political beliefs and those of the managerial interests I mentioned just now are almost identical. Our resources are immense, but we need men. A man.

BITOS. (*Still suspicious*) I don't think I understand you quite, my dear Brassac.

BRASSAC. (*The captain of men, very debonair suddenly*) Why don't you telephone me one morning at the factory and we'll have a chat about it over lunch? I'll tell you the details of a cherished plan of mine. Our syndicate is thinking of creating a job which would ensure contact between the various departmental heads and technical groups on the one hand, and the masses on the other—whole sections of which we are quite unable to reach. A sort of People's Representative, with the most extensive powers—and nothing to prevent it from expanding subsequently to national level. . . .

He has refilled BITOS' *glass as he speaks.*

BITOS. (*Sipping his drink musingly*) But my functions as an official of the courts forbid me to—

BRASSAC. (*Expansively*) My dear fellow. The courts, like everything else, are made to be got out of.

He taps him smartly on the shoulder, as if every-

*thing were already signed and sealed. Then he
becomes bland again.*
But we'll talk about it all later. We're boring these lovely
ladies. We're supposed to be enjoying ourselves!
*He claps his hands cheerfully and gathers them
closer.*
Friends! Why don't we all go to the Pink Eagle? They say
the new band is very good.

MAXIME. Brilliant idea! (*Calling*) Charles!

BITOS. (*Suddenly skittish*) The Pink Eagle? I'm told it's a
very . . . frisky sort of place. I don't know if I can allow
myself, in my capacity as a magistrate—

BRASSAC. (*Confidentially*) My dear fellow, you'll find them
there to a man. But there's an unwritten rule, everybody
pretends not to recognize anybody else.

BITOS. (*Clucking*) I must say they've made quite an art of
these little niceties in your set. . . .
He drains his glass.
And very pleasant too!
A heavy knock is heard. CHARLES *goes up the
stairs, opens the door and talks to somebody
outside.*

CHARLES. M. Maxime, there's a man here who says he wants
M. Bitos.

JULIEN. (*Pretending to panic*) It's Fessard! Hide me! He's
going to ask me for money!

AMANDA. (*Clapping her hands*) Is it the friend? The famous
garageman? Do persuade him to come with us. He'll be
such fun!

BITOS. (*Purring*) No, no, ladies. He really is too crude. (*To*
CHARLES) Convey my thanks, my good man, and tell him
everything is all right now.

CHARLES. It might be better if you appeared in person, sir. He
seems very worried about you, sir.

BITOS. (*Animatedly*) Dear, dear, dear, how absurd! One second, gentlemen. I'll just send him away and then I'm all yours.

> He goes quickly up the stairs, reeling a little, and disappears into the street, calling in his falsetto voice:

Fessard!

MAXIME. (*Between his teeth*) It's superb! Superb! My dear Brassac, it's better than I ever dreamed! You're a genius!

BRASSAC. (*Smiling modestly as he lights a cigar*) Of sorts, yes. What will you bet that he telephones the factory within two days to ask me to ask him to lunch?

MAXIME. And will you?

BRASSAC. (*Softly, into his cigar*) I won't.

> JULIEN *steps forward, drunk, powerful, malevolent.*

JULIEN. So we ship this son of the people to the Pink Eagle, right? I must say I'm feeling in great form. I've an itch in the toe of my boot. You should never have let me get a sniff of that Bitos. I absolutely must kill some pauper meat tonight. I'm sick to death of hearing them cry "Misery me!" as soon as they've eaten their sausage. Sick of it! Death to the weak! Death to the poor and needy!

> He takes them by the arm, his eyes glinting.

My friends, you leave Bitos to me at the Pink Eagle. I'll pick a quarrel with him—over Lea, for instance, who's bound to be there, she is every night. And this time, I'll smash him. And it won't even be an insult to a magistrate. It will be a settling of accounts between two drunkards, over a whore! Give me another drink.

MAXIME. Julien, you're drunk.

JULIEN. (*Helping himself*) Not quite!

VICTOIRE. (*Going to* MAXIME) Maxime, I really think I must go home now. I'm not going to that place with you.

MAXIME. (*Kissing her hand affectionately*) You're right, my little pet. It's certain to turn squalid. I'll drop you on the way.

VULTURNE. I'm going home, too, Maxime. I'll drop Victoire.

MAXIME. (*With a hard smile*) I thought you would. I've never persuaded you to stay to the end of a bullfight either.

VULTURNE. (*Quietly*) I don't like to see anything killed. A shot at a bird on the wing, all right. But to watch a cornered animal waiting . . .

MAXIME. (*Laughing*) Your Grace, there must have been a little hiatus in your lineage. Some amorous young tutor and a great grandmama with time on her hands.

VULTURNE. (*Smiles and says quietly, as he goes up the stairs*) This will surprise you. I rather wish that sometimes . . .
> BITOS *reappears, in great form, and shouts down the stairs.*

BITOS. There! The bumpkin has gone. Poor lad, he came with his apprentice, both of them armed to the teeth and ready to save my life. (*He splutters with mirth*) He wouldn't go, you know! It was priceless! He kept on saying "Are you sure you're not letting yourself in for anything, M. Bitos?" (*He wheezes with laughter*)

BRASSAC. (*Patting him on the back and giving him a cigar*) A severe hangover, at the very most! (*In his ear*) Or an affair. Our little Amanda has her eye on you, do you know that?

BITOS. (*Very much the man about town, puffing at his huge cigar*) Easy, is she?

BRASSAC. When she likes you!

MAXIME. Come along, everybody, quickly. We'll take all four cars. (*Calling*) Charles! The coats!

CHARLES. (*Panicking*) Is everybody leaving at once?

MAXIME. (*Laughing*) Yes, everybody! Hurry up, man.

CHARLES. (*Distressed*) What about dinner? I've kept everything hot!

MAXIME. (*Putting on his coat*) You two eat it. Eat till you
burst!

CHARLES. (*Calling into the kitchen*) Joseph, help! Bring the
cloaks! They're all leaving in a bunch again.

> *The coats are handed around, the guests go up
> the stairs again—one of them opens the door
> and looks at the weather.*

LILA. (*From upstairs*) The rain's quite stopped. It's a wonderful night.

> BITOS *has put on his Robespierre jacket. He now
> gallantly helps* AMANDA *on with her things.*

BITOS. Long live the nighttime, lovely lady. It's funny, I'm
not used to staying up late. Everything feels different at
night.

> *He is about to go up the stairs with the last guests.
> Then an anxious look crosses his face, he puts his
> hand inside his coat and calls discreetly to*
> MAXIME *as the others go out.*

My dear Maxime, a stupid accident . . . I think I've split
the seat of my breeches.

> *He makes sure they are alone and feels his behind
> to learn the worst.*

How silly. I shan't be able to go to that club with you.

MAXIME. Nonsense. Charles! Would you do M. Bitos a small
service? A case of mending the seat of his trousers, he's
split them. Discreetly, I'm relying on you.

CHARLES. I'll do my best, M. Maxime.

> *He hurries out.*

MAXIME. We'll wait for you in the car, Bitos. A little more
whisky to help you through the operation?

BITOS. (*Simpering*) I'm going too far this evening, far too far.
All that drink, this cigar . . .

MAXIME. (*Suddenly unaccountably grave*) There are certain

evenings when however far one goes, one never goes too far. Make haste, Charles.

> *He goes out.* BITOS *remains alone with* CHARLES.

CHARLES. (*Calling after* MAXIME) I'll be as quick as I can, sir. (*To* BITOS) If you'd be so good as to remove your overcoat, sir, it would be easier.

> BITOS *takes off his coat. He is standing in the middle of the room, smoking his cigar.* CHARLES, *crouching behind him, is sewing up his rear.*

BITOS. I'm very worried about this costume. I borrowed it from the local theatre. They made me pay a very exhorbitant deposit.

> *A short pause. He adds anxiously:*

I hope they'll give it back to me.

CHARLES. (*Doubtfully*) Well, of course, with this tear . . . You can always point out that the seat was very ripe, sir.

BITOS. An old castoff, and they hired the thing out at an outrageous price. It did suit me, though, didn't it?

CHARLES. (*Politely*) You looked very smart indeed in it, sir. Excuse me, sir, but if you would kindly stick out your posterior, sir, it would make the stitching easier.

> BITOS *sticks out his behind.*

CHARLES. Thank you, sir. That's just right. It gives the stuff a bit of body, as you might say.

> VICTOIRE, *who had left with the others, suddenly appears at the top of the stairs and asks, bewildered:*

VICTOIRE. Why, what are you doing?

BITOS. (*Straightening in panic, his hand on his behind*) Mlle. de Brèmes! That was unworthy of you! . . . a stupid accident . . . I've split the seat of my trousers. It's very mean of you to spy on me like that.

VICTOIRE. (*Gently*) I wanted to talk to you.

BITOS. (*Who goes on clutching his rear throughout the scene*)

After what happened with your father this afternoon we have nothing further to say to each other. Anyway, you could have spoken to me over at that club.

VICTOIRE. I'm not going. (*To* CHARLES) Charles, could you leave us for two minutes? What I have to say to M. Bitos won't take very long.

CHARLES. Very good, mademoiselle. Perhaps you will call me? *He goes out.* BITOS *is still standing very stiff and still, his hand on his behind, without looking at her.* VICTOIRE *has come right down the stairs. A horn hoots for them out in the street, then stops.*

VICTOIRE. (*Suddenly quietly*) You mustn't go to that night club with them, M. Bitos.

BITOS. (*Aggressively*) Is that your business?

VICTOIRE. (*Gently*) Yes.
A short pause. She adds:
They're still planning to make a fool of you.

BITOS. (*Still truculently, without venturing to meet her eyes*) Aren't I old enough to see that for myself, if it's true?

VICTOIRE. (*With the ghost of a smile*) No. I don't think you are.

BITOS. (*With a sudden bark*) Do you think I'm some sort of an idiot?

VICTOIRE. (*Gravely*) I don't love you, M. Bitos. That's why your proposal this afternoon was unacceptable.

BITOS. Your father threw me out like a common thief!

VICTOIRE. (*Gently*) I beg your pardon for what my father did. . . . If you had spoken to me I would simply have told you that you were mistaken and I couldn't love you. . . . For a girl's reasons, which have nothing to do with what you are in the world. (*She smiles kindly*) You know, there have been a lot of girls who didn't want to marry a man and who told him so. These are small wounds and one forgets them. . . . (*She goes on, more gravely*) Don't go with them tonight, M. Bitos. They'll give you wounds of a different sort and you won't recover from those so easily. They're taking you there so they can make fun of you.

BITOS. (*With a terse cackle*) Am I so funny?
> *The hooters sound again.*

VICTOIRE. You must believe me. Quickly, we haven't much time. They only flattered you so as to destroy you. The proposition Brassac made is probably only a game to get you to make a fool of yourself. But even if he meant it, it would be shameful.
> *A pause.*

BITOS. (*Heavily*) What do you know about it?

VICTOIRE. (*Gently*) I don't love you. I could never love a man like you. But I think there's a kind of true courage, a kind of steely worth in you. . . . Don't go to that night club with them and have still more to drink. . . . (*She smiles kindly*) In the first place, you can't drink . . .

BITOS. (*Cackling ironically as he pulls at his cigar*) Indeed?
> *He unfortunately hiccups at the same time. He throws away his cigar with a shudder of disgust.*

VICTOIRE. (*Goes on, kindly*) Don't go with them to be laughed at, don't go to Lila's to play the social lion, which you're very bad at. Stay yourself. Stay poor.
> *A little pause. She adds:*

The only thing I could have loved about you, if I could have loved you, was your poverty. But like all precious things, poverty is very fragile. Keep yours intact, M. Bitos. And never forget that your family crest has your mother's two red arms on it—crossed.
> *She repeats the little gesture he made earlier in the play when speaking of his mother. She looks at him and smiles.* BITOS *is very pale. He stands there, silent, frightening, motionless. Suddenly, he stops clutching his behind and picks up his little black overcoat, swiftly puts it on and sets*

> *his bowler on his head, his face set and drawn.*
> *The car hooters have started up again outside.*

BITOS. (*Between his teeth*) Very well, I'll go out the back way.

> *In the kitchen doorway he turns, lifts up his coat*
> *collar and mutters icily:*

Thank you, mademoiselle, for this little homily. You've saved me from making a blunder. (*He adds heavily*) But if I can ever get my own back on you all one day, you are the one I shall start with.

> *He goes out. She has not moved. One can still*
> *hear the hooters calling outside. She murmurs:*

VICTOIRE. Poor Bitos . . .

> *And she goes swiftly up the stairs. The curtain*
> *falls as she goes out amid the din of the car*
> *hooters, which have all started up together this*
> *time.*

CURTAIN